AAT

Ethics for Accountants

Level 3
Advanced Diploma in
Accounting
Course Book

Third edition 2018

ISBN 9781 5097 1833 7
ISBN (for internal use only) 9781 5097 1827 6

British Library Cataloguing-in-Publication Data
A catalogue record for this book is available from the British Library

Published by

BPP Learning Media Ltd
BPP House, Aldine Place
142-144 Uxbridge Road
London W12 8AA

www.bpp.com/learningmedia

Printed in the United Kingdom

Your learning materials, published by BPP Learning Media
Ltd, are printed on paper obtained from traceable
sustainable sources.

BPP
LEARNING MEDIA

Contents

Introduction to the course

Syllabus overview

This unit is about professional ethics in an accounting environment. It seeks to ensure that students need to act ethically, of the principles of ethical working of what is meant be ethical behaviour at work, and of when and how to take action in relation to unethical behaviour and illegal acts.

This unit supports students in:

- Working within the ethical code applicable to accountants and accounting technicians

- Ensuring that the public has a good level of confidence in accounting practices or functions

- Protecting their own and their organisation's professional reputation and legal liability

- Upholding principles of sustainability.

Students will learn the core aspects of the ethical code for accountants as it relates to their work as accounting technicians and as exemplified in the AAT *Code of Professional Ethics*. They will understand the ethical principles of integrity, objectivity, professional competence and due care, and professional behaviour and confidentiality, and they will learn to apply these principles to analyse and judge ethical situations at work.

They will also understand that acting ethically derives from core personal and organisational values, such as honesty, transparency and fairness, as well as from professional ethics. Understanding the conceptual framework of principles, threats and safeguards contained in the ethical code, plus its process for ethical conflict resolution, will enable students to apply a systematic approach to ethical problems that they may encounter.

In studying this unit, students will therefore develop skills in analysing problems and in judging between 'right' and 'wrong' behaviour in a given context. They will also be able to identify alternative courses of action to resolve an ethical problem and select the most appropriate action in the circumstances.

Money laundering regulations mean that accountants can be exposed to legal liability for keeping quiet in certain circumstances or for telling the wrong person about suspected wrongdoing. Students will learn when and how money laundering regulations apply and their responsibilities in respect of them. They will also learn about reporting to the authorities in respect of suspected money laundering. In certain other circumstances, it may be appropriate for an accountant to report, 'speak up' or blow the whistle on unethical behaviour.

Finally, students will understand the basis and nature of the accountant's ethical responsibilities to uphold sustainability in their organisation.

Test specification for the Level 3 synoptic assessment – Ethics for Accountants, Advanced Bookkeeping, Final Accounts Preparation, Management Accounting: Costing and Spreadsheets for Accounting

Test specification for this unit assessment

Assessment method	Marking type	Duration of assessment
Computer based synoptic assessment	Partially computer / partially human marked	3 hours (including 15 minutes for uploading work) consisting of two parts

Learning outcomes for Ethics for Accountants
1   Understand the need to act ethically
2   Understand the relevance to the accountant's work of the ethical code for professional accountants
3   Recognise how to act ethically in an accounting role
4   Identify action to take in relation to unethical behaviour or illegal acts

Assessment objectives for the Level 3 synoptic assessment	Weighting
1 Demonstrate an understanding of the relevance of the ethical code for accountants, the need to act ethically in a given situation, and the appropriate action to take in reporting questionable behaviour	15%
2 Prepare accounting records and respond to errors, omissions and other concerns, in accordance with accounting and ethical principles and relevant regulations	15%
3 Apply ethical and accounting principles when preparing final accounts for different types of organisation, develop ethical courses of action and communicate relevant information effectively	15%
4 Use relevant spreadsheet skills to analyse, interpret and report management accounting data	25%
5 Prepare financial accounting information, compromising extended trial balances and final accounts for sole traders and partnerships, using spreadsheets	30%
Total	**100%**

Assessment structure

3 hours duration (including 15 minutes for uploading work)

Competency is 70%

*Note that this is only a guideline as to what might come up. The format and content of each task may vary from what we have listed below.

Your assessment will consist of 5 tasks.

Task	Expected content	Max marks	Unit ref	Study complete
Task 1.1	**How to act ethically and the importance of the code for professional accountants. Identification of actions to take for unethical behaviour or illegal acts.** The style of this task can include picklists, drag and drop and gapfill entry.	15	This task will be assessed on content from the Ethics for Accountants unit	
Task 1.2	**Recognise to act ethically and identify actions to take. Apply various advanced bookkeeping skills and show an understanding the need for final accounts and prepare accounting records from incomplete information.** The style of this task can include picklists, drag and drop, gapfill entry and ticks.	15	This task will be assessed on content from the following units: Ethics for Accountants, Advanced Bookkeeping and Final Accounts Preparation	
Task 1.3	**Recognise how to act ethically in an accounting role. Distinguish between financial recording and reporting requirements for different organisations including limited companies and sole traders.** It is likely the style of this task will be a written response in the form of a report, memo, note or email	15	This task will be assessed on content from the following units: Ethics for accountants and Final Accounts Preparation	

Task	Expected content	Max marks	Unit ref	Study complete
Task 2.1	**A range of spreadsheet skills to analyse, interpret and report management accounting data.** This task will be completed using spreadsheet software.	25	This task will be assessed on content from the following units: Management Accounting: Costing and Spreadsheets for Accounting	
Task 2.2	**Prepare financial information, comprising of extended trial balances and final accounts for sole traders and partnerships.** This task will be completed using spreadsheet software.	30	This task will be assessed on content from the following units: Final Accounts Preparation and Advanced Bookkeeping	

Skills bank

Our experience of preparing students for this type of assessment suggests that to obtain competency, you will need to develop a number of key skills.

What do I need to know to do well in the assessment?

Ethics for Accountants is part of the Level 3 synoptic assessment. It is designed to cover the professional ethics requirements on the other assessment units on this synoptic.

To be successful in the ethics objectives of the assessment you need to:

- Understand the ethical principles and identify any threats to the principles
- Understand that ethics derives from personal and organisational values
- Be able to identify appropriate conflict resolution processes
- Be able to apply a systematic approach to ethical problems

Assumed knowledge

If you have studied AAT at Level 2 then the following topics were studied in *Work Effectively in Finance* and are also relevant to this synoptic assessment:

- **Continuing professional development** – *Ethics for Accountants* builds upon the requirement of finance professions to keep up-to-date in skills and knowledge to help ensure workplace tasks are completed with competency.

- **Sustainability and corporate social responsibility** – The importance supporting sustainability and organisations acknowledging a social responsibility is expanded upon in *Ethics for Accountants*.

- **Confidentiality and honesty** – These two areas form part of the ethical principles and are an essential part of the Level 3 synoptic assessment.

You can see that several topics were already introduced in *Work effectively in finance*. The most important thing to do, though, is to re-visit your understanding of any ethical concepts that you have covered before your *Ethics for Accountants* course starts.

Assessment style

In the assessment you will complete tasks by:

1. Entering narrative by selecting from drop down menus of narrative options known as **picklists**

2. Using **drag and drop** menus to enter narrative

3. Typing in numbers, known as **gapfill** entry

4. Entering **ticks**

5. Entering **dates** by selecting from a calendar

6. **Writing** answers

7. Using **spreadsheet** software

You must familiarise yourself with the style of the online questions and the AAT software before taking the assessment. As part of your revision, login to the **AAT website** and attempt their **online practice assessments**.

Answering written questions

In your assessment there will be written questions on ethical principles, potential threats to those principles and appropriate actions to take. The main verbs used for these types of question requirements, are as follows, along with their meaning:

Identify – Analyse and select for presentation.

Explain – Set out in detail the meaning of an ethical situation.

Discuss – By argument, discuss the pros and cons.

Analysing the scenario

Before answering the question set, you need to carefully review the scenario given in order to consider what questions need to be answered, and what needs to be discussed. A simple framework that could be used to answer the question is as follows:

* Point – Make the point.
* Evidence – Use information from the scenario as evidence.
* Explain – Explain why the evidence links to the point.

For example, if an assessment task asked us to explain how fraud would impact on ethics we could answer as follows:

1 Point – Theft breaches the integrity principle due to a threat of self-interest and is also a criminal offence.

2 Evidence – An accountant is making unauthorised cash withdrawals from a business bank account.

3 Explain – This means the accountant may receive a criminal conviction and will bring the accountancy profession into disrepute.

Recommendations are normally also required, and to provide guidance on how to proceed:

1 Recommendation – Therefore the action we should take is to report any suspicion or evidence of theft to our supervisor and/or to the relevant authorities.

This approach provides a formula or framework that can be followed, to answer written questions:

Theft breaches the (Point)....an accountant is making (Evidence)....this means the accountant is (Explain)....therefore the action we should take (Recommendation).

Introduction to the Level 3 synoptic assessment

The question practice you do will prepare you for the format of tasks you will see in the *Ethics for Accountants* part of the assessment. It is also useful to familiarise yourself with the introductory information you **may** be given at the start of the assessment. For example:

Assessment information

- Read the scenario carefully before attempting the questions; you can return to it at any time by clicking on the 'Introduction' button at the bottom of the screen.

- Complete all 5 tasks.

- Answer the questions in the spaces provided. For answers requiring free text entry, the box will expand to fit your answer.

- You must use a full stop to indicate a decimal point. For example, write 100.57 **not** 100,57 or 100 57.

- Both minus signs and brackets can be used to indicate negative numbers **unless** task instructions say otherwise.

- You may use a comma to indicate a number in the thousands, but you don't have to. For example, 10000 and 10,000 are both acceptable.

- Where the date is relevant, it is given in the task data.

- **Tasks 1.1 to 1.3** in **Section 1** require you to enter your answer in the assessment environment.
  Tasks 2.1 to 2.2 in **Section 2** require you to download files and work outside the assessment environment in a spreadsheet software program.

  You should ensure that you have uploaded all files required before you finish and submit the assessment.

Information

- The total time for this paper is 3 hours (including 15 minutes for uploading work).

- This assessment has a total of **5 tasks** which are divided into subtasks across two sections.

- The total mark for this paper is 100.

- The marks for each sub-task are shown alongside the task.

- The data you need to complete a task is contained within that task or through the pop-up that appears on the task page; you will not need to refer to your answers for previous tasks.

---

1   As you revise, use the **BPP Passcards** to consolidate your knowledge. They are a pocket-sized revision tool, perfect for packing in that last-minute revision.

2   Attempt as many tasks as possible in the **Synoptic Question Bank**. There are plenty of assessment-style tasks which are excellent preparation for the real assessment.

3   Always **check** through your own answers as you will in the real assessment, before looking at the solutions in the back of the Question Bank.

Key to icons

	Key term	A key definition which is important to be aware of for the assessment
	Formula to learn	A formula you will need to learn as it will not be provided in the assessment
	Formula provided	A formula which is provided within the assessment and generally available as a pop-up on screen
	Activity	An example which allows you to apply your knowledge to the technique covered in the Course Book. The solution is provided at the end of the chapter
	Illustration	A worked example which can be used to review and see how an assessment question could be answered
	Assessment focus point	A high priority point for the assessment
	Open book reference	Where use of an open book will be allowed for the assessment
	Real life examples	A practical real life scenario

AAT qualifications

The material in this book may support the following AAT qualifications:

AAT Advanced Diploma in Accounting Level 3, AAT Advanced Diploma in Accounting at SCQF Level 6.

Supplements

From time to time we may need to publish supplementary materials to one of our titles. This can be for a variety of reasons, from a small change in the AAT unit guidance to new legislation coming into effect between editions.

You should check our supplements page regularly for anything that may affect your learning materials. All supplements are available free of charge on our supplements page on our website at:

www.bpp.com/learning-media/about/students

Improving material and removing errors

There is a constant need to update and enhance our study materials in line with both regulatory changes and new insights into the assessments.

From our team of authors BPP appoints a subject expert to update and improve these materials for each new edition.

Their updated draft is subsequently technically checked by another author and from time to time non-technically checked by a proof reader.

We are very keen to remove as many numerical errors and narrative typos as we can but given the volume of detailed information being changed in a short space of time we know that a few errors will sometimes get through our net.

We apologise in advance for any inconvenience that an error might cause. We continue to look for new ways to improve these study materials and would welcome your suggestions. Please feel free to contact our AAT Head of Programme at nisarahmed@bpp.com if you have any suggestions for us.

These learning materials are based on the qualification specification released by the AAT in April 2018.

BPP
LEARNING MEDIA

The principles of ethical working

1

Learning outcomes

1.1	**Explain why it is important to act ethically**

Students need to know:

- The effect of an accountant acting ethically on the level of confidence that the public has in all accountants, on the probity and reputation of the accountant's organisation and on the accountant's own professional reputation and legal liability
- The importance of an accountant complying with the ethical code at all times
- About the accountant's public interest duty to society as well as to the client or employer
- About the ethical code's objective of maintaining the reputation of accountancy as a profession
- About the legal and professional nature of the accountant's obligation of compliance with the ethical code
- About consequences for members of professional accountancy bodies who breach their ethical codes
- When disciplinary action by the relevant professional accountancy body may be brought against the accountant for misconduct, and the possible penalties that can arise
- When internal disciplinary procedures may be brought against the accountant by the employer for unethical or illegal behaviour
- About fines or reputational damage suffered by organisations as a result of unethical behaviour and non-compliance with values, codes and regulations

1.2	**Explain how to act ethically**

Students need to know:

- About specific actions that the accountant may have to take in order to behave ethically
- Why simply complying with regulations may not constitute ethical behaviour, depending on the circumstances
- Why a methodical approach to resolving ethical problems is advisable
- How the ethical code takes a principles-based not a rules-based approach to ethics, conduct and practice

1.3	Explain the importance of values, culture and codes of practice/conduct
	Students need to know:
	• How an organisation's values, corporate culture and leadership affect its decisions and actions
	• Why conflict may arise and have to be resolved between an individual's key personal values and organisational values
	• The importance of an ethics-based culture and ethical leadership within an organisation
	• How codes of conduct, codes of practice and regulations may affect ethical decisions by organisations and individuals
2.1	Explain the ethical code's conceptual framework of principles, threats, safeguards and professional judgement
	Students need to know:
	• The importance of an accountant evaluating threats to compliance with the fundamental principles and then implementing safeguards, using professional judgement, to eliminate the threats or reduce them to an acceptable level
	• The types of threat to the fundamental principles
	• The types of safeguard that may be applied
	• How documented organisational policies on various issues can be used as safeguards to prevent threats and ethical conflict from arising
	• What an accountant should do when a threat cannot be eliminated or reduced to an acceptable level
2.2	Explain the importance of acting with integrity
	Students need to know:
	• The meaning of integrity from the ethical code
	• The effect of accountants being associated with misleading information
	• The meaning of the key ethical values of honesty, transparency and fairness
	• The importance of acting at all times with integrity, honesty, transparency and fairness when liaising with clients, suppliers and colleagues
	• How integrity is threatened in particular by self-interest and familiarity threats
2.3	Explain the importance of objectivity
	Students need to know:
	• The meaning of objectivity from the ethical code
	• The importance of maintaining a professional distance between professional duties and personal life at all times
	• The importance of appearing to be objective as well as actually being objective
	• The importance of professional scepticism when exercising professional judgement
	• How accountants may deal with offers of gifts and hospitality
	• How objectivity is threatened in particular by intimidation, self-review and advocacy threats as well as by self-interest and familiarity threats

2.4	**Explain the importance of behaving professionally**
	Students need to know:
	• The meaning of professional behaviour from the ethical code
	• How the ethical code as a whole sets out the required standards of behaviour for accountants and how to achieve them
	• How compliance with relevant laws and regulations is a minimum requirement
	• Why an act that is permitted by the law or regulations is not necessarily ethical
	• The link between bringing disrepute on the profession may in itself lead to disciplinary action by a professional accountancy body
	• How professional behaviour is threatened in particular by self-interest, self-review and familiarity threats
2.5	**Explain the importance of being competent and acting with due care**
	Students need to know:
	• The meaning of professional competence and of due care from the ethical code
	• How professional qualifications and continuing professional development (CPD) support professional competence
	• The areas in which up-to-date technical knowledge may be critical to an accountant's competence
	• How professional competence and due care are threatened in particular by self-interest, self-review and familiarity threats
2.6	**Explain the importance of confidentiality and when confidential information may be disclosed**
	Students need to know:
	• The meaning of confidentiality from the ethical code
	• The types of situation that present threats to confidentiality
	• How confidentiality is threatened in particular by self-interest, intimidation and familiarity threats
3.1	**Distinguish between ethical and unethical behaviour**
	Students need to be able to:
	• Apply values and principles to identify whether behaviour is ethical or unethical in a given situation
	• Apply key organisational values to a given situation, including complying with regulations in spirit as well as letter, with regard to: being transparent with customers and suppliers; reporting financial and regulatory information clearly and on time; whether to accept and give gifts and hospitality; paying suppliers a fair price and on time; providing fair treatment, decent wages and good working conditions to employees; using social media
	• Identify situations where there is pressure to behave unethically, especially from self-interest, familiarity and intimidation threats to the fundamental principles

3.5	**Explain the ethical responsibilities of accountants in upholding the principles of sustainability**
	Students need to know:
	• The meaning of sustainability
	• The importance of considering the needs of the organisation's wider stakeholders
	• The importance of taking a long-term view and allowing the needs of present generations to be met without compromising the ability of future generations to meet their own needs
	• The link between sustainability and the accountant's ethical principle of integrity
	• The links between the accountant's public interest duty to protect society as a whole and the organisation's sustainability
	• The importance of: social and environmental aspects of performance measurement and decision-making techniques; long-term responsible management and use of resources; operating sustainably in relation to products and services, customers, employees, the workplace, the supply chain and business functions and processes

Assessment context

The **fundamental ethical principles** underpin acting ethically and in the assessment you will need to identify principles and also identify how they may be threatened. In addition the assessment can include working within the legal and regulatory framework and the importance of the AAT *Code of Professional Ethics*.

Qualification context

In ethics for accountants you will develop an understanding of the importance of fulfilling the ethical duties you have to undertake as an AAT accountant. This is a fundamental part of your skill set and is a critical part in upholding the AAT qualification.

Business context

Behaving ethically is of paramount importance to you as an individual and to the profession as a whole. Accountants should be operating in the interests of the public. Whether you are working in practice or in business you are working to the same principles. There have been a number of scandals over the years that have tainted the public perception of the profession. Enron is a notorious example of a company which pushed the boundaries and ultimately became famous for all the wrong reasons.

Chapter overview

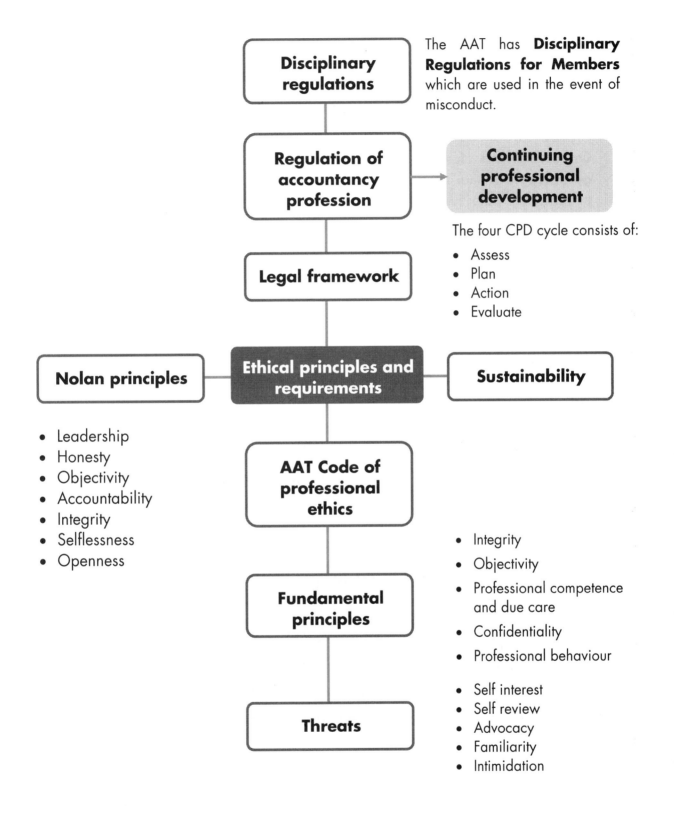

Disciplinary regulations

The AAT has **Disciplinary Regulations for Members** which are used in the event of misconduct.

Regulation of accountancy profession

Continuing professional development

The four CPD cycle consists of:
- Assess
- Plan
- Action
- Evaluate

Legal framework

Nolan principles

Ethical principles and requirements

Sustainability

- Leadership
- Honesty
- Objectivity
- Accountability
- Integrity
- Selflessness
- Openness

AAT Code of professional ethics

- Integrity
- Objectivity
- Professional competence and due care
- Confidentiality
- Professional behaviour

Fundamental principles

- Self interest
- Self review
- Advocacy
- Familiarity
- Intimidation

Threats

Introduction

Ethics are a set of moral principles that guide behaviour and **ethical values are** assumptions and beliefs about what constitutes 'right' and 'wrong' behaviour. Ethical values are often linked to our own **personal values** and these can include loyalty to friends, family and employers, and showing fairness and respect to others that we meet in our daily lives.

Individuals have **personal ethics**, often reflecting the beliefs of the families, cultures and educational **environments** in which they developed their ideas.

Organisations also have ethical values, based on the **norms and standards of behaviour** that their leaders believe best help them express their identity and achieve their objectives.

The concept of business ethics suggests that businesses are morally responsible for their actions and should be held accountable for them.

Accountants work in the public interest. This means they have a duty to society as a whole, and therefore strong moral values are essential to the profession.

Ethical behaviour has an increasingly important part to play in our everyday lives and before moving on to the section have a think about what behaving ethically can mean to you as an AAT student and as an accountant.

The role of the accountant

Before we look at professional ethics in detail it is important to consider the role of the accountant.

Accountants are generally employed in **three main areas**: in practice, in a business or in the public sector.

Accountants in **practice** will provide services for a number of clients, for example to produce final accounts and tax returns.

An accountant who works in **business** is employed to perform work for the organisation that employs them, for example producing financial accountants for external users or management accounts used by the senior management team.

Accountants in the **public sector** perform similar roles to those employed in business however the difference is that their employer will be a public service organisation, such as the health service or local government.

The wide variety of work that can be performed by accountants can put them at risk from different ethical dilemmas.

Illustration 1: An ethical dilemma

Denis is an accountant working in practice and one of her clients requests her to prepare a financial reference that will be used to support a bank loan. Denis is fully aware that the client's business is in serious financial trouble and without the loan will be unable to continue to trade and many jobs will be lost. She shows the client a draft financial reference that has been prepared and the client requests that some figures are to be restated to show the business in a more favourable light.

How do you feel Denis should react to this request? Should Denis take into account the job losses or does she have responsibility to the bank, the accountancy profession and the wider public to report the true picture?

This is an example of an ethical conflict. Although potential job losses would be a concern for Denis this should not affect her objectivity in completing the client's bank reference. Although Denis will have a duty to her client, she will also have a professional duty to the bank, her professional body and the wider community to complete the work with the correct figures. If the bank relied upon misleading figures this could result in a wrong decision being reached. This can bring financial problems for parties relying on this finance including disrepute for Denis and the accountancy profession.

If there are to be job losses then Denis may be able to offer some advice to her client on how the redundancies can be managed in the most ethical way.

1 AAT Code of Professional Ethics

Key term

The AAT requires their members and students to adopt and maintain high ethical standards. To assist with this they have published the **AAT Code of Professional Ethics**. This is available on the AAT website (www.aat.org.uk) and AAT members are required to act in accordance with the Code.

The **AAT (2017)** has the AAT **Code of Professional Ethics** (The AAT Code) and its purpose is to set out the required standards of professional behaviour with guidance on how these standards can be achieved.

The AAT *Code of Professional Ethics* came into effect on 1 September 2011 and the most recent revision of it came into force on 15 July 2017.

The AAT are keen that students are familiar with the Code as this will assist in their professional roles. However, the information needed specifically for the exam is included in this Course Book.

Note that the emphasis of the exam is on the practical application of the Code. Therefore section number references will not be tested in the assessment.

The AAT *Code of Professional Ethics* is split into 3 parts and these are divided into sub-sections for each area of guidance.

Section	Title	Application
Part A	General application of the Code	Applies to all members
Part B	Members in practice	Applies to members in practice
Part C	Members in business	Applies to members in business

Essentially, a **member in practice** provides accountancy, taxation or related consultancy services **to another business** on a self-employed basis.

A **member in business** is someone who is **employed** by a company, the public sector or the not–for–profit sector.

1.1 Why have a 'Code' of professional ethics?'

The AAT could have taken a **rules-based** approach to ethics. This would have involved creating a large book of rules, trying to cover every possible ethical scenario that could be faced, with an answer to every single ethical problem.

In the modern day business environment it would be very difficult to include rules on all situations a member may encounter. There would also be scope for manipulating the rules.

So instead, the AAT *Code of Professional Ethics* adopts a **principles-based** approach. This principles-based approach allows the individual to decide what behaviour is appropriate and to **exercise professional judgement** on a case-by-case basis.

A code is designed to give guidance on what behaviour is considered ethical. It is not legally binding but gives advice on how to comply with the law.

Under the AAT *Code of Professional Ethics*, as a minimum you are expected to comply with the laws and regulations of the country in which you live and work.

In addition the AAT (like other professional bodies) requires its members to behave in a way that maintains its **reputation, maintains public confidence** and **protects the public interest**. This benefits the AAT, its members, the wider accounting profession, employers and society as a whole.

Many industries introduce their own codes of conduct and practice to regulate the activities of member businesses and individuals. Industry codes are often voluntary, but some have a statutory basis and are legally binding. Non-compliance with codes not only damages the reputation of organisations but can also result in fines for unethical or illegal behaviour.

Activity 1: Benefits and drawbacks of following the AAT *Code of Professional Ethics*

The ethical code exists in order to improve the accountancy profession and its public image.

Required

Identify the benefits and drawbacks of an accountant following the AAT *Code of Professional Ethics* by ticking the relevant column.

Description	Benefit ✓	Drawback ✓
Cost of increased work		
Restriction on services you can provide		
Job satisfaction		
Better reputation		
Increased workload		
Protection from negligence claims		

1.2 Business ethics

Businesses have a duty to act in the best interests of society as a whole and so the idea behind business ethics is that businesses are morally responsible for their actions.

The importance of business values in a company's culture is that they underpin both policy and behaviour throughout the company, from top to bottom.

A consequence of the need for a business to act ethically is for it to change its culture so that all employees, managers and directors know what is expected of them. This can be achieved through active leadership by setting the **'tone at the top'** approach where senior management and executives lead by example.

Businesses often aim to act competitively and maximise profit. However, there is a distinction between **competing aggressively** and **competing unethically** (eg spreading false, negative information about competitors).

The Institute of Business Ethics (IBE) encourages high standards of ethical behaviour in businesses.

The Institute of Business Ethics website (www.ibe.org.uk) suggests ethical tests for a business decision:

Transparency	Do I mind others knowing what I have decided?
Effect	Who does my decision affect or hurt?
Fairness	Would my decision be considered fair by those affected?

Activity 2: Ethical tests of effect

One of the Institute of Business Ethics' (IBE) simple ethical tests for a business decision is related to effect.

Required

Complete the following sentence by selecting the appropriate option.

When considering effect, the employee will ask himself or herself:

	▼

Picklist:

Do I mind others knowing what I have decided?
Who does my decision affect or hurt?
Would my decision be considered fair by those affected?

2 Legal framework

All individuals and organisations are expected to accept and obey the law. Compliance with the law is the minimum level of behaviour expected by society and is a base from which ethics and professional rules of behaviour are built on. This is sometimes referred to as the **law is a floor** and meeting legal requirements will protect an accountant's legal liability. Although, complying with the law may not necessarily mean someone is acting ethically.

In the UK, law falls into two categories and these are **criminal law** offences and **civil law** conflicts.

	Criminal law	**Civil law**
Type of behaviour	Offences relating to persons or property that affect the whole community	Wrongs relating to conflicts between individuals within the community
Examples	Money laundering or fraud	Breach of contract, negligence
Court	Criminal cases are prosecuted in a criminal court	Civil cases are heard in a civil court
Consequences	Individual is liable to the state; fines or imprisonment	Remedies are designed to place the injured party in the position they would be in were it not for the breach

2.1 Breach of contract

If a member in practice provides services to a client, those services should be performed with reasonable skill and care.

If the member fails to exercise reasonable skill and care they may be liable to the client for breach of contract and professional negligence.

This breach of contract or negligence is, of course, between the individuals involved and not the state.

Tort is different from a liability arising from a breach of contract. Where one person owes a duty of care to another, they must exercise reasonable skill and care. They do **not** have to have entered into a contractual relationship.

For example, if a solicitor is asked to draft a will naming certain beneficiaries, but does so negligently meaning that the intended beneficiaries do not inherit, the solicitor may be liable in tort to the intended beneficiaries even though there was no contract between them.

2.2 Laws and regulations affecting the accountancy profession

There are a number of other **laws and regulations** affecting the accountancy and finance sector, and business in general.

While you do not need to know the details of these laws, for the exam you need to be aware of them where they are relevant to the accountancy profession.

Examples of such laws are:

- Health and safety legislation
- Employment law
- Environmental legislation

We must comply with the law and regulations. However, ethics is a refinement of that behaviour. There are many actions that are unethical but not illegal.

Activity 3: Unethical but not illegal

Can you suggest actions or behaviour that may be unethical but not illegal?

Activity 4: Code of Ethics – true or false?

Are the statements below true or false?

Required

Answer the question by ticking the appropriate boxes.

Statement	True ✓	False ✓
The AAT *Code of Professional Ethics* is legally enforceable.		
The AAT *Code of Professional Ethics* is an example of criminal law.		
Breach of the AAT *Code of Professional Ethics* on the marketing of professional services will give an AAT member a criminal record.		

Activity 5: Internal code of conduct

An accountancy practice has prepared an internal code of conduct to assist staff in their day-to-day working life.

Suggest possible content that could be included in the internal code to meet this objective.

3 Regulation of the accountancy profession

Before we look at the detail of the AAT *Code of Professional Ethics* it is useful to understand where it sits within the accountancy world.

The International Federation of Accountants (IFAC) is an international body representing all the major accountancy bodies across the world. Its mission is to develop the high standards of professional accountants.

International Ethics Standards Board for Accountants (IESBA)

To assist with this, IFAC's ethics committee (the IESBA) publishes a **Code of Ethics for Professional Accountants**. All the main accountancy bodies comply with its principles.

Consultative Committee of Accountancy Bodies (CCAB)

The major chartered accountancy bodies joined together to form the CCAB. It provides a forum for matters affecting the profession to be discussed, and enables members to speak with a unified voice.

The current members are:

Professional body	Initials
Institute of Chartered Accountants in England and Wales	ICAEW *
Institute of Chartered Accountants in Scotland	ICAS *
Institute of Chartered Accountants in Ireland	ICAI
The Association of Chartered Certified Accountants	ACCA
The Chartered Institute of Public Finance and Accountancy	CIPFA *

* Three professional bodies in the CCAB sponsor the AAT. They are the ICAEW, ICAS and CIPFA.

The fourth professional body that sponsors the AAT is the Chartered Institute of Management Accountants (CIMA).

The AAT itself is not part of the CCAB. It is vocational; members are accounting technicians who have practical accounting skills for use in the workplace.

The Financial Reporting Council (FRC)

The FRC regulates the accountancy and actuarial professions. It aims to promote ethical financial reporting and increased confidence in the accountancy profession in the UK. The responsibilities of the FRC include issuing standards for corporate reporting, audit & assurance, and actuarial work. The FRC monitors and enforces compliance with regulations and standards and any non-compliance can result in disciplinary action.

The FRC also issues its own FRC *Ethical Standard*, which supplements the IESBA *Code of ethics* with its own requirements.

Activity 6: Sponsoring bodies

Required

Complete the table by selecting the appropriate option from the choices below.

(a) Which of the following bodies sponsors the AAT?

Organisation	✓
ICAS	
ACCA	
FRC	
CIPFA	

(b) Which of the following statements are true of the Financial Reporting Council (FRC)?

Statement	✓
The FRC regulates the global accountancy profession.	
The FRC issues standards for professionals involved in audit and assurance work.	
The FRC has the authority to discipline accountants who do not observe actuarial standards.	

There are other bodies you need to be aware of and these can include the following.

HM Revenue & Customs (HMRC)

You will be familiar with HMRC! It is a government department and its aim is to ensure that the correct tax is paid at the right time.

National Crime Agency (NCA)

The **National Crime Agency (NCA)** is a government department and its aim is to tackle serious organised crime that affects the United Kingdom and its citizens. Serious organised crime includes:

- Class A drugs
- Human trafficking
- Fraud
- Money laundering

For your assessment you need to know about the role of NCA in addressing money laundering. This is discussed in a later chapter.

4 Fundamental ethical principles

The accountancy profession could have taken a **rules-based** approach to ethics. Instead, the AAT *Code of Professional Ethics* adopts a **principles-based** approach.

The AAT *Code of Professional Ethics* (AAT, 2017) has five **fundamental ethical principles** which underpin ethical behaviour in an accounting context:

Fundamental principle	Explanation
Integrity	A member shall 'be straightforward and honest in all professional and business relationships.' (AAT, 2017: p.9)
Objectivity	A member 'shall not allow bias, conflict of interest or undue influence of others to override professional or business judgements.' (AAT, 2017: p.9)
Professional competence and due care	Members must 'maintain professional knowledge and skill at the level required to ensure that clients or employers receive a competent professional service ... [They must] act diligently when providing professional services.' (AAT, 2017: p.9)
Confidentiality	Members must 'not disclose information acquired as a result of professional and business relationships unless there is a legal or professional right or duty to disclose.' (AAT, 2017: p.9) Confidential information must not be used to the advantage of members or third parties.
Professional behaviour	Members must avoid any action that may bring disrepute to the profession.

Here are the five ethical principles in further detail:

Integrity

The principle of integrity requires all members to be 'straightforward and honest in business and professional relationships.' (AAT, 2017: p.13) This implies 'fair dealing and truthfulness.' (AAT, 2017: p.13)

The AAT Code (2014) requires members not to be associated with reports, returns and communications or other information that they believe is false, misleading, supplied carelessly or omits or obscures information where such omissions or obscurity would be misleading.

On an everyday level, integrity involves matters such as being open about limitations of knowledge and competence, being honest in your relationships and carrying out your work accurately, conscientiously and efficiently.

Objectivity

The AAT Code (2017) states that 'the principle of objectivity imposes an obligation on all members not to compromise their professional or business judgement because of bias, conflict of interest or the undue influence of others.' (p.14)

Professional judgement can also include the use of professional scepticism when considering whether objectivity has been compromised in any way.

Members should not only be objective but also be seen as objective from the view of third parties. This can mean considering how the receipt of gifts or hospitality can be seen by others in threatening a member's objectivity.

Professional competence and due care

Professional competence and due care means that having agreed to perform a task you have an obligation to perform it:

- To the best of your ability
- In the client or employer's best interests
- Within a reasonable timescale
- With regard to the technical and professional standards expected of you as a professional

The AAT Code requires members to act diligently in accordance with those technical and professional standards.

Members are required to keep up to date in skills and knowledge by completing **continuing professional development** to support professional competence.

Failing to work with professional competence and due care can result in accusations of professional negligence and breach of contract.

In addition there can be criminal accusations of fraud and money laundering if the accountant is not up to date with legislation and regulations.

Members should make clients and employers aware of any limitations in their skills or knowledge as carrying out tasks beyond skills or training would be seen as careless and even negligent.

Confidentiality

The AAT Code (2017) defines the principle of confidentiality as imposing an obligation on members to refrain from:

- **Disclosing confidential information** outside the firm or employing organisation without proper and specific authority unless there is a legal or professional right to do so.
- **Using confidential information** to their personal advantage or the advantage of third parties.

When looking at confidentiality members need to take into account data protection laws (such as the Data Protection Act), as information can be restricted or protected by legislation as well as ethical guidelines.

There are circumstances where the law allows or requires confidentiality to be breached.

These are summarised below.

Circumstance	Examples
'Disclosure is permitted by law and is authorised by the client or the employer' (AAT, 2017: p.15)	Providing working papers to a new firm who is taking on the client
Disclosure is 'required by law'. (AAT, 2017: p.15)	Providing documents for legal proceedings Disclosure to Her Majesty's Revenue & Customs (HMRC) in relation to taxation matters Disclosure of actual or suspected money laundering activities to the firm's Money Laundering Reporting Officer (MLRO) or to the National Crime Agency (NCA) in the UK
There is a professional right or duty to disclose when it is in the public interest and is not prohibited by law.	Compliance with a quality review by a professional body Responding to an enquiry or investigation by the AAT or other regulatory or professional body Disclosure to protect the member's professional interests in legal proceedings

Professional behaviour

The AAT Code (2017) states that 'the principle of professional behaviour imposes an obligation on members to comply with relevant laws and regulations and avoid any action that may bring disrepute to the profession' (AAT, 2017: p.16).

Behaviour that reflects badly on the reputation and standing of the AAT can result in disciplinary action taken against the member.

Applying the professional behaviour principle means 'being professional' and this can include:

- As a minimum, complying with the law

- Behaving in a way to maintain or enhance the reputation of the profession

- Behaving with courtesy and consideration towards anyone you come into contact with professionally and in your personal life

Assessment focus point

In your assessment you could be asked to identify and explain one or more ethical fundamental principles. Therefore it is **very important** you understand the meaning of the five principles and how they can relate to specific ethical situations. When approaching a written task make use of the information given looking for any factors that may be unethical to include in your answer. Always **explain** and give **reasons** for your suggestions. For example, 'Confidentiality has been breached here **because** unauthorised staff had access to the password' or 'The accountant has breached professional behaviour **as** he/she has brought disrepute onto the profession due to his/her unethical actions'

The following activity provides an opportunity to consider the meaning of each of the five fundamental ethical principles in practical illustrations.

Activity 7: Fundamental ethical principles and scenarios

Explain the fundamental principle that is most relevant to each of the following scenarios.

Scenario	Fundamental principle and explanation
Tom is a journalist who writes articles for a financial newspaper and has been recommending his readers to purchase shares in companies that he holds shares in.	
A member of a professional body has been caught speeding while driving to a client meeting. The speeding offence has been reporting in the local media naming both the member's name and professional body membership.	
Toni is a junior member of staff and has been requested to complete a complex sales ledger reconciliation. Normally, the work should take two days, however Toni has been allocated one morning to complete the work.	

Scenario	Fundamental principle and explanation
A partner in a firm of accountants has spent 40 hours working on a client's financial statements. Before an invoice is sent to the client the partner notices that 80 hours have been used for the invoice calculation. The partner allows the invoice to be sent based on 80 hours instead of 40 hours.	
Jackie is an accountant specialising in tax dispute cases. As a marketing initiative Jackie has posted details of successful cases on her accountancy practice website. To help with authenticity Jackie has used the real names of past and present clients without their permission.	

5 The conceptual framework

It is impossible to give guidelines on every possible situation that may arise in the course of your work which conflicts with the fundamental principles. The ethical code therefore sets out a basic conflict resolution process that can assist in complying with the principles. This procedure forms the **conceptual framework** which requires the following:

- **Identify** where there may be a threat to a fundamental principle.

- **Evaluate** the threat. How significant is it?

- For any significant **threats** apply safeguards to eliminate or reduce the threat.

- If safeguards cannot be applied, decline or discontinue the professional service involved and this may mean resigning from an assignment or employment.

Members are also encouraged to seek external advice on areas of conflict and one example here can be contacting the AAT for guidance on the most appropriate action to take in specific ethical circumstances.

6 Threats to fundamental ethical principles

Compliance with the principles may be **threatened** in business and in practice by any number of **threats**.

Most threats fit into the following categories:

Threat	Explanation
Self interest	'May occur where a financial or other interest will inappropriately influence the member's judgement or behaviour' (AAT, 2017: p.11)
Self-review	'May occur when a previous judgement needs to be re-evaluated by the member responsible for that judgement' (AAT, 2017: p.11)
Advocacy	'May occur when a member promotes a position or opinion to the point that subsequent objectivity may be compromised' (AAT, 2017: p.11)
Familiarity	'May occur when, because of a close or personal relationship, a member becomes too sympathetic to the interests of others' (AAT, 2017: p.11)
Intimidation	'May occur when a member may be deterred from acting objectively by threats, whether actual or perceived' (AAT, 2017: p.11)

It is important to note that not all threats are capable of being categorised in this way. If you come across such a threat, it is important not to ignore it, but deal with it the best you can.

In your assessment you may be given a scenario and asked to identify the type of threat that is illustrated.

Activity 8: Threats to the fundamental principles

Explain the threat that is most relevant to each of the following scenarios:

Scenario	Ethical threat and explanation
Steve is a member in practice. He is currently engaged on an assurance assignment with Potter plc. On Sunday he celebrated his successful completion of his AAT training. As a gift his grandmother has transferred her 2% shareholding in Potter plc to him.	
The accountant at JED has been taken ill. JED's audit firm has been asked to prepare the financial statements and audit the financial statements.	
Charles Greenfield has been the engagement partner on the audit of Hamptons for many years.	

6.1 Safeguards to threats

The AAT Code (2017) defines safeguards as 'actions or other measures that may eliminate threats or reduce them to an acceptable level' (p.11). This means that a safeguard is something you can do when you encounter a threat.

The Code identifies two broad categories of safeguards that you might use to reduce or eliminate the threats.

Safeguards created by the profession and/or legislation and regulation. These include:

- Education, training and continuing professional development (CPD)
- Corporate governance regulations
- Professional standards
- Professional or regulatory monitoring
- Disciplinary procedures
- External review of financial reports, returns and other communications

Safeguards in the work environment. These include:

- Quality controls and internal audit procedures
- Mechanisms to protect and empower staff ('whistleblowing')
- Consultation with third parties
- Rotation of personnel
- Use of ethic committees or forums
- Organisational policies to document threats
- Use of professional judgement

Activity 9: Identifying threats to the ethical principles

In this activity you will need to identify and discuss which ethical principle is being threatened in each of the six matters.

Background information:

Garden centres – matter 1

This is a limited company, which operates a chain of garden centres specialising in the selling of high quality exotic plants and landscaping services. The only shareholders of the company are two brothers who also manage the centres on a day-to-day basis. As they are approaching retirement age they have decided to sell the company and move to Spain.

One of the brothers has approached you as a local experienced accountant and requested that you prepare a valuation of the company. They have always trusted you with their tax affairs as they have limited knowledge of finance and tax.

Your main area of expertise is preparing tax returns for the many IT consultants that have sprung up in your town. However, you have long admired their business and often considered acquiring part ownership in something similar. The likely sale of the company seems like an ideal opportunity for you (with your business partners) to enter the gardening trade.

You have been told that your valuation will be the likely starting point in any negotiations with potential buyers.

Hair salon – matter 2

This is a local business in a small parade of shops in which your accounting firm is situated. Parking has always been difficult in the area and recently the hair salon owner next door proposed that they convert the land at the back of the shops, in which they all have joint ownership, into a car park that could be used by customers and clients. They have offered to arrange everything and then invoice each shop owner for their share which was agreed at the outset through a complex split based on the number of customers each shop expects in a typical week.

You know from being a customer of the hair salon in the past that their record keeping is not of a high quality and that they are at risk of going out of business.

Your firm is sent an invoice for £1,500 and pays the hair salon owner. You request a copy of the invoice from the builder for your firm's records. On receipt of the copied invoice you note that you have been undercharged per the split of costs that was agreed. In fact your share should have been £2,100.

Software developer – matter 3

A local millionaire who has been very successful at developing new educational software has arranged to meet with you. He wants to discuss plans for future investments and has asked you to bring along ideas for how he should best invest his very substantial cash holdings. He is not risk averse and has always considered himself to be a bit of an opportunist.

You have another client who is looking for an investor in his property company. You have always enjoyed working with this client and often play golf at the weekends. Indeed, both of your families have been on holiday to Disneyland together.

Your team mate – matter 4

You play football on Saturday morning with a group of friends. One of them approaches you after a particularly exhausting training session and asks for your advice about claiming back VAT for a not-for-profit organisation of which he is a director.

Your father-in-law – matter 5

Your father-in-law has seen his pension fund fall in value recently and has put off retiring for a few years. He has recently started work at a company on a very good salary for which you prepare the financial statements.

You are aware that the company has performed poorly in the last financial year, and there may be questions over whether the current year financial statements can be prepared on a going concern basis.

Your plumber – matter 6

A plumber has given you a quote for a job at your house and has suggested that if you were to pay in cash he could give you a discount equivalent to the current rate of VAT.

Required

For each of the following situations identify and explain the ethical issues.

- Garden centres
- Hair salon
- Software developer
- Your team mate
- Your father-in-law
- Your plumber

---

7 Nolan principles

The Committee on Standards in Public Life is an advisory body of the UK government. It was established in response to concerns that conduct by some politicians was unethical.

A report by the Nolan Committee established **The Seven Principles of Public Life**. They are relevant to accountants as there are some similarities with the AAT's fundamental principles.

The seven principles are:

(1) Leadership
(2) Honesty
(3) Objectivity
(4) Accountability
(5) Integrity
(6) Selflessness
(7) Openness

(Committee on Standards in Public Life, 1995)

(This phrase should help you to remember them: **L**iz **H**urley **O**nly **A**rgued **I**f **S**he **O**bjected.)

These are the principles we would expect holders of public office to take into consideration in their actions in public life. This is topical in light of the scandals surrounding the global banking crisis, UK MPs' expenses and the ongoing argument over bankers' bonuses.

Leadership

'Holders of public office should challenge poor behaviour when it occurs' (Committee on Standards in Public Life, 1995).

Honesty

'Holders of public office should be truthful' (Committee on Standards in Public Life, 1995).

Objectivity

Decisions should be taken impartially, fairly on merit 'without discrimination or bias' (Committee on Standards in Public Life, 1995).

Accountability

Holders of public office are accountable for decisions and actions, and are subject to scrutiny.

Integrity

Individuals should not place themselves under any financial or other obligation to third parties that might seek to influence them in performance of their duties.

Selflessness

'Holders of public office should act solely in terms of the public interest' (Committee on Standards in Public Life, 1995).

Openness

Decisions should be taken 'in an open and transparent manner' (Committee on Standards in Public Life, 1995) unless there are clear reasons for not doing so.

Activity 10: Identifying the Nolan Principles

The **Nolan principles** are relevant to accountants as there are some similarities with the AAT's fundamental principles.

Required

Identify the Nolan principle being described by selecting the appropriate principle from the picklist.

Description	Principle
Holders of public office should be as open as possible about all the decisions and actions that they take. They should give reasons for their decisions.	▼
Holders of public office should not place themselves under any financial or other obligation to outside individuals or organisations that might seek to influence them in the performance of their official duties.	▼
Holders of public office have a duty to declare any private interests relating to their public duties and take steps to resolve any conflicts arising in a way that protects the public interest.	▼
Holders of public office should promote and support these principles by leadership and example.	▼

Description	Principle
Holders of public office are accountable for their decisions and actions. They must submit themselves to whatever scrutiny is appropriate to their office.	▼
Holders of public office should act solely in terms of the public interest. They should not do so in order to gain financial or other material benefit for themselves, their family or their friends.	▼
In carrying out public business (eg making public appointments, recommending individuals for rewards and benefits), holders of public office should make choices on merit.	▼

Picklist:

Accountability
Honesty
Integrity
Leadership
Objectivity
Openness
Selflessness

8 Operational risk

There are a number of risks associated with doing business. A particularly important risk is **operational risk.**

The **Basel Committee on Banking Supervision (BCBS) (2011)** defines **operational risk** as 'the risk of loss resulting from inadequate or failed processes, people and systems or from external events' (p.3).

Operational risks arise from the daily functions of a business. The definition is very broad and can include the risk of:

- Fraud – internal and external
- Business disruption
- Employment practices
- Process and delivery risks
- Reputational risk
- Legal risks
- Physical and
- Environmental risks

An organisation will have a process of risk management for each area of the business. Operational failure can cause significant damage to a business. It is important to understand that some of the factors that contribute to something going wrong in how an organisation conducts its business can be controlled to some extent by codes of conduct and an ethical programme.

According to the Basel Committee (2011) the following specific risk areas present the potential for events that represent an operational risk.

Activity 11: Types of operational risk

Identify the type of operational risks for each of the following examples:

Example	Type of operational risk
Misappropriation of assets	
Theft of information	
Discrimination	
Knowingly selling products with defects	
Vandalism	
Using pirated software that contains bugs	
Inaccurate or misleading reporting	
Loss of confidence by the public	
Damages paid to customers for injury caused by a faulty product	

9 Disciplinary regulations

There are consequences for AAT members who do not comply with the codes of practice and regulations.

The AAT has a set of Disciplinary Regulations (2016) for members which are used in the event of misconduct.

Essentially, there are grounds for disciplinary action if a member conducts themselves in a manner that prejudices their status as a member or reflects adversely on the reputation of the AAT.

The following events are conclusive proof of misconduct (AAT, 2016):

(i) A member pleads guilty to or has been found guilty of an indictable criminal offence.

(ii) A member becomes bankrupt or enters into any formal arrangement with their creditors.

(iii) A member has not complied with the Money Laundering Regulations.

(iv) A member has not complied with the AAT's CPD requirements.

(v) A member unreasonably refuses to co-operate with an investigation into their conduct.

(vi) A member in practice has failed to renew his/her practising licence before expiry.

(vii) A member repeatedly failed to reply to AAT correspondence.

The disciplinary process

Minor breaches of the AAT *Code of Professional Ethics*, which do not amount to misconduct, are dealt with under **informal procedures**. This involves contacting the member, informing them of the breach and advising them of any steps they should take to correct it.

Other complaints may be resolved by **conciliation**.

There is then a five-stage **standard procedure** (AAT, 2016) which is used for complaints not resolved by informal procedures or conciliation. The standard procedure is as follows:

Stage 1	Disciplinary investigation to establish the facts
Stage 2	Decision and recommendation as to whether there are grounds for action
Stage 3	Member's response to those recommendations
Stage 4	Preliminary matters and pre-hearing protocol
Stage 5	Disciplinary tribunal to hear submissions and witnesses

The following disciplinary actions may be recommended for a member who is found guilty of misconduct:

- Be expelled from the Association
- Have his/her membership suspended
- Have his/her practising licence withdrawn
- Be declared ineligible for a practising licence
- Have his/her fellow member status removed
- Be severely reprimanded
- Be fined
- Receive a written warning

If a member is guilty of misconduct then it is likely they are in breach of their employer's internal disciplinary rules as well.

Activity 12: Misconduct investigation

Harrison is a full member of the AAT. He is being investigated for misconduct.

Required

Identify whether each of the following circumstances are conclusive proof of Harrison's misconduct under the AAT's Disciplinary Regulations by ticking the appropriate option.

Circumstance	Conclusive proof of misconduct ✓	Not conclusive proof of misconduct ✓
Harrison unreasonably refused to co-operate with an investigation into his conduct.		
Harrison failed to reply to correspondence from the AAT on one occasion.		

If an accountant's actions are sufficient for them to be disciplined by their professional body then it is likely that they may be in breach of their employer's internal disciplinary rules as well. Punishment will depend on the severity of the behaviour. Minor issues can result in an informal or formal warning. Major breaches of discipline, such as theft, may result in them losing their job.

10 Continuing professional development (CPD)

As we have seen a fundamental principle is professional competence and due care.

The AAT requires all members to participate in continuing professional development (CPD) to maintain their **professional competence**.

There are a number of factors that may influence the CPD undertaken by a member:

- Introduction of new software or equipment
- Skills shortfalls identified by the member as they work
- Feedback from managers
- Business/professional developments

There are lots of resources available for CPD, such as courses and seminars, books, professional publications, downloads and websites. Members should use the resource most suitable for their needs and learning preferences.

Each AAT member must complete the four-step CPD cycle at least once in a 12-month period (twice for members in practice). This four-step cycle consists of:

Step 1	**Assessing** your learning and development needs for the year (or half-year) ahead
Step 2	**Planning** the learning activity
Step 3	Putting the learning plan into **action**
Step 4	**Evaluating** the outcomes at the end of the year (or half-year)

Members must keep adequate CPD records so they can demonstrate they have complied with the AAT's CPD policy.

CPD is a safeguard created by the profession to help manage threats to the fundamental principles.

Activity 13: The AAT CPD Cycle

Required

Complete the following sentence by selecting the appropriate option.

The AAT's CPD cycle comprises four steps: assess, [▼], action and evaluate.

Picklist:

consider
decide
discuss
plan

Activity 14: CPD in practice

(a) Accountants are required to undertake continuing professional development (CPD).

Required

State TWO of the fundamental principles that can be safeguarded by CPD.

(b) Edward is a professional accountant and is a sole practitioner. Many of Edward's clients are small incorporated businesses and some trade on a cash-only basis. In addition to financial statement preparation Edward also offers a tax return completion service for his clients.

Required

What areas of technical knowledge should Edward keep up to date with?

11 Sustainability and corporate social responsibility (CSR)

Accountants are expected to act and protect the public interest and in the modern business world this means that **sustainable development** and **corporate social responsibility** are becoming increasingly important.

Sustainable development means that an organisation should develop its operation to co-exist with society and this can be achieved by putting the long-term future ahead of short-term gains.

Accountants also have a **corporate and social responsibility (CSR)** to promote **sustainability**. This means that accountants are accountable for their social and ethical effects of their actions. This responsibility includes being transparent and open on their sustainability policies. Accountants have a **public interest** duty to protect society as a whole. This means that accountants have a wider responsibility towards sustainability extending beyond the office environment.

A company's CSR can be defined as the **obligations** that it feels it has to its local community, persons and organisations connected to it and to society as a whole. For example, organisations that source materials from developing countries may feel they should pay a fair price for the goods that they buy.

Two definitions of sustainability

Goldsmith and Samson (2005) 'a long-term programme involving a series of sustainable development practices, aimed at improving organisational efficiency, stakeholder support and market edge'

World Commission on Environment and Development (1987) 'sustainability means taking a long-term view and allowing the needs of present generations to be met, without compromising the ability of future generations to meet their own needs' Extract from Our Common Future commonly referred to as the UN's Brundtland Report

Duties of finance professionals

Sustainability is often associated with protecting the environment and 'green' issues, however finance professionals have broader duties in respect of economic (financial) and social issues. This can mean ensuring that business models are financially sustainable. Companies such as Kodak and Nokia had superb business models but due to lack of vision and research and development lost their market positions. Socially, finance professionals can help with sustainability by encouraging employing locally and ensuring the workforce is trained to meet future business developments.

The diagram below shows how economic (financial), social and environmental responsibilities are interlinked and this is sometimes referred to as a **triple bottom line** approach. Economic (financial), environmental and social responsibilities assist finance professionals to look beyond the traditional financial reporting framework of looking solely at the net profit figure or only the 'bottom line' results.

Other responsibilities linked to sustainability can include:

- Paying suppliers a fair price for goods and services
- Paying suppliers on time
- Good working conditions for employees and paying decent wages
- Taking into account the views of the local community when making decisions
- Being transparent with customers and suppliers
- Using social media in an ethical manner

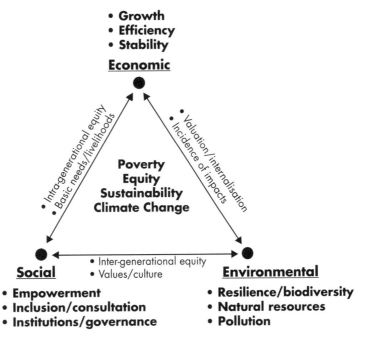

Activity 15: Triple bottom line model

Jack is an accounting technician working in practice. His manager has read something in the press about corporate social responsibility and has asked Jack to give examples of how an accountancy firm could meet these responsibilities.

How could Jack respond?

	Possible suggestions
Economic (financial)	
Social	
Environmental	

Risks of not acting sustainably

There are a number of risks to the organisation and society of not acting sustainably. As resources are used up and get scarcer, their price will rise and so will the manufacturing organisation's costs. Acting sustainably now may prevent or delay such price rises. For example, batteries use lithium which is a finite resource. With the increased use in portable communication devices has resulted in increased costs. However, as a potential sustainable solution manufacturers who use this resource are looking into alternative power methods.

For society, the lack of sustainability now may mean fewer products in the future as the resources used to make them are used up. Damage from pollution may become irreversible and lead to long-term changes to the planet.

Responsibilities of finance professionals

There are six main responsibilities for finance professionals in upholding the principles of sustainability

1	Creating and promoting an ethical culture
2	Championing the aims of sustainability
3	Evaluating and quantifying reputational and other ethical risks
4	Taking social, environmental and ethical factors into account when making decisions
5	Promoting sustainable practices, for example fair treatment of employees
6	Raising awareness of social responsibility

Focus on the key words: creating and promoting, championing, evaluating, decisions, practices and raising awareness. (This phrase should help you remember them: **C**aptain **P**ugwash **C**an **E**asily **D**rive **P**irates **R**apidly **A**way.)

It is important to recognise that accountants have a responsibility to act in the public interest and have wider social responsibilities not just confined to the office environment.

Activity 16: Suggestions for sustainability

One of your accounting firm's newest fully qualified professional accountants, Jamie, is very keen to promote sustainability development in the firm. Jamie has made a presentation to the firm's staff which mentions that accountants are obliged to support and develop sustainability.

Required

Describe five ways in which an accountancy practice can seek to support sustainability and sustainable development within the firm.

- **Ethical values** are assumptions and beliefs about what constitutes 'right' and 'wrong' behaviour. Individuals, families, national cultures and organisation cultures all develop ethical values and norms.

- **Ethical behaviour** is necessary to comply with laws and regulations; to protect the public interest; to protect the reputation and standing of a professional body and its members; and to enable people to live and work together in society.

- **The five fundamental principles** of accountants are:
  - Integrity
  - Objectivity
  - Professional competence and due care
  - Confidentiality
  - Professional behaviour

- The ethical code sets out a **basic conflict-solving process** for unethical action (the 'conceptual framework'):
  - Identify the threat to the fundamental principles that the action represents
  - Evaluate the threat
  - Apply safeguards to eliminate or reduce the threat
  - If safeguards cannot be applied, decline or discontinue the action

- The **principles-based approach** to ethics encourages case-by-case judgement.

- The accountancy profession is largely self-regulatory, with the professional accountancy bodies each responsible for setting and upholding the ethical standards of their members. This chapter looked at the roles of:
  - FRC
  - IFAC
  - CCAB
  - HMRC
  - NCA

- A **code of conduct** is designed to influence the behaviour of employees; it sets out the procedures to be used in specific ethical situations.

- A **code of practice** is adopted by a profession or organisation to regulate that profession.

- The concept of **business ethics** suggests that businesses and other corporate entities are morally responsible for their actions.

- Finance professionals have a duty to protect the **public interest** and promote **sustainability**. They should consider the **economic (financial)**, **social** and **environmental aspects** to their work.

- As part of their role, finance professionals have a number of **responsibilities** in relation to upholding the principles of **sustainability**.

- There are a number of **operational risks** that businesses face, such as reputation, litigation, process, people, systems, legal and event risk. Many of these risks are affected by unethical behaviour.

- An accountant that is found to have committed **misconduct** is liable for a fine or expulsion from their professional body as well as sanctions from their employer.

- **Continuing professional development** activities ensure that you maintain your technical and professional competence, keeping pace with changes in your work role and the practices, techniques and standards of your profession.

- **Civil law:** Relates to legal conflicts between individuals and organisations within the whole community; there is no state involvement and so imprisonment is not a possible punishment

- **Code of professional ethics:** A code adopted by a profession or organisation to provide clear guidance to members on what behaviour is considered ethical

- **Conceptual framework:** An approach that can assist in problem solving in many different situations

- **Continuing professional development (CPD):** A process of continuously maintaining and developing knowledge, skills and competence

- **Corporate and social responsibility (CSR):** Where companies are accountable for the social and ethical effects of their actions

- **Criminal law:** Relates to offences against persons or property that affect the whole community. There is state involvement and imprisonment is a possible punishment

- **Financial Reporting Council (FRC):** The UK's independent regulator of the accountancy and actuarial professions

- **Fundamental ethical principles:** There are five fundamental ethical principles and they are: integrity, objectivity, professional competence and due care, confidentiality and professional behaviour

- **National Crime Agency (NCA):** An agency that tackles and investigates serious crime within the UK

- **Nolan principles:** Seven principles that should apply to public life, which are: integrity, objectivity, accountability, openness, leadership, selflessness and honesty

- **Operational risk:** Risks to an organisation that can cause loss or damage by faulty internal systems or staff or as a consequence of other, external events

- **Sponsoring bodies:** Accountancy bodies that sponsor the AAT; they include ICAEW, ICAS and CIPFA

- **Sustainable development:** An approach where an organisation works alongside society and looks to the long term

- **Threats:** An identifiable risk or risks to the five fundamental principles

- **Triple bottom line model:** Identification of sustainability aspects under economic (financial), social and environmental factors

Test your learning

1   Respond to the following by selecting the appropriate option.

Only individuals can have 'ethical values'.

	✓
True	
False	

2   The accountancy profession needs to maintain standards of conduct and service among its members in order to be able to:

	✓
Enhance the reputation and standing of accountants	
Limit the number of members that it has	
Make sure that accountants are able to earn large salaries	

3   Which of these might (or might be thought to) affect the objectivity of providers of professional accounting services?

	✓
Failure to keep up to date on CPD	
A personal financial interest in the client's affairs	
Being negligent or reckless with the accuracy of the information provided to the client	

4   A client asks you a technical question about accounting standards which you are not sure you are able to answer correctly. 'You are supposed to be an accountant, aren't you?' says the client. 'I need an answer now.' What should you do first?

	✓
Say that you will get back to him when you have looked up the answer.	
Give him the contact details of a friend in your firm who knows all about accounting standards.	
Clarify the limits of your expertise with the client.	

5   Put the four steps of the problem-solving methodology or 'conceptual framework' for ethical conduct into the correct order.

Apply safeguards to eliminate or reduce the threat to an acceptable level.	▼
Evaluate the seriousness of the threat.	▼
Discontinue the action or relationship giving rise to the threat.	▼
Identify a potential threat to a fundamental ethical principle.	▼

Picklist:

1
2
3
4

6   Why are professional standards important?

	✓
It is in the public interest that accountants who fail to comply with standards are prosecuted.	
It is in the public interest that accountancy services are carried out to professional standards.	

7   Which of the following could be considered safeguards against threats to the fundamental ethical principles?

	✓
Rotation of personnel	
Having an employee share scheme	
Use of ethic committees	
Use of professional judgement	
Encouraging staff to cycle to work	

8   What are the three aspects of the triple bottom line model?

	✓
Economic (financial)	
Marketing	
Environmental	
Charity	
Social	
Political	

9   Which type of operational risk can be defined as a risk of losses from human error or deliberate actions?

	✓
Reputational	
Litigation	
Process	
People	
Systems	
Legal	
Event	

10   An accountant is expected to keep themselves up to date in all aspects of accountancy, even in areas outside their area of work.

	✓
True	
False	

Behaving in an ethical manner – part I

2

Learning outcomes

2.2	**Explain the importance of acting with integrity**
	Students need to know:
	• The meaning of integrity from the ethical code
	• The effect of accountants being associated with misleading information
	• The meaning of the key ethical values of honesty, transparency and fairness
	• The importance of acting at all times with integrity, honesty, transparency and fairness when liaising with clients, suppliers and colleagues
	• How integrity is threatened in particular by self-interest and familiarity threats
2.3	**Explain the importance of objectivity**
	Students need to know:
	• The meaning of objectivity from the ethical code
	• The importance of maintaining a professional distance between professional duties and personal life at all times
	• What is meant by a conflict of interest, including self-interest threats arising from financial interests, compensation and incentives linked to financial reporting and decision making
	• The importance of appearing to be objective as well as actually being objective
	• The importance of professional scepticism when exercising professional judgement
	• How objectivity is threatened in particular by intimidation, self-review and advocacy threats as well as by self-interest and familiarity threats
2.5	**Explain the importance of being competent and acting with due care**
	Students need to know:
	• The meaning of professional competence and of due care from the ethical code
	• How professional qualifications and continuing professional development (CPD) support professional competence
	• The areas in which up-to-date technical knowledge for an accountant's competence may be critical
	• How professional competence and due care are threatened in particular by self-interest, self-review and familiarity threats

2.6	**Explain the importance of confidentiality and when confidential information may be disclosed**
	Students need to know:
	• The meaning of confidentiality from the ethical code
	• The types of situation that present threats to confidentiality
	• How confidentiality is threatened in particular by self-interest, intimidation and familiarity threats
3.2	**Analyse a situation using the conceptual framework and the conflict resolution process**
	Students need to be able to:
	• Apply the conceptual framework to a situation
	• Apply the conflict resolution process to a situation
	• Decide when to take advice externally
	• Decide when to refuse to remain associated with the matter creating the conflict, or resign

Assessment context

In this chapter we will look specifically at how to behave in an ethical manner when working as a member in practice or a member in business. In the assessment you may be presented with various ethical threats and asked to identify the type of threat being illustrated. You could then be required to suggest appropriate safeguards to manage the threat.

Qualification context

When working in a business environment you should be aware of the potential threats to the fundamental principles and the safeguards available to you.

Business context

Organisations need to recognise the risks facing them in the current business environment and be vigilant when carrying out day-to-day activities. Globalisation has opened up many opportunities but along with this there are significant threats.

Chapter overview

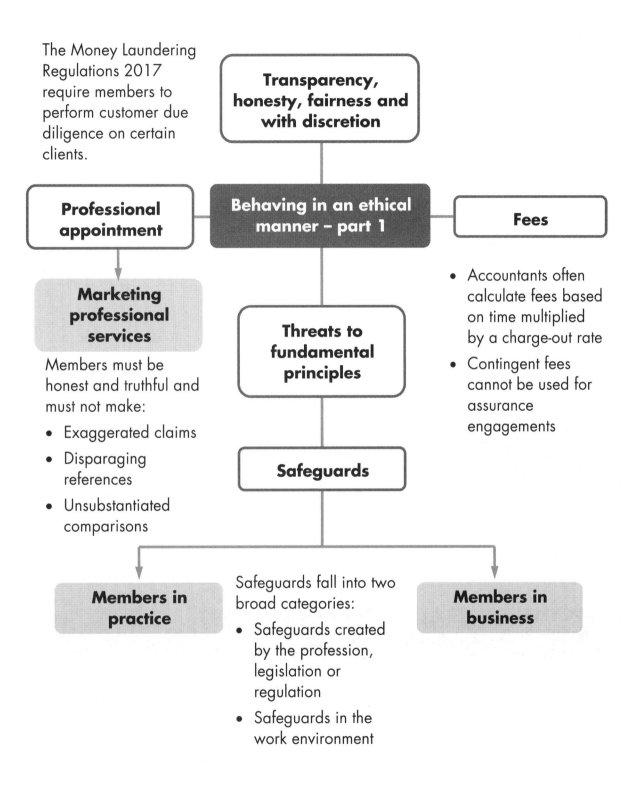

The Money Laundering Regulations 2017 require members to perform customer due diligence on certain clients.

Transparency, honesty, fairness and with discretion

Professional appointment

Behaving in an ethical manner – part 1

Fees

Marketing professional services

Members must be honest and truthful and must not make:

- Exaggerated claims
- Disparaging references
- Unsubstantiated comparisons

Threats to fundamental principles

- Accountants often calculate fees based on time multiplied by a charge-out rate
- Contingent fees cannot be used for assurance engagements

Safeguards

Members in practice

Safeguards fall into two broad categories:

- Safeguards created by the profession, legislation or regulation
- Safeguards in the work environment

Members in business

Introduction

Accounting matters often require the use of personal and professional judgement, and opinions as to the best or 'right' way to handle them can often differ. Moreover, people need to develop their own ethical and technical judgement, as part of their own personal and continuing professional development.

In this chapter we will look at what behaving ethically means in practice beginning with acting with integrity, honesty, fairness and sensitivity in dealings with clients, suppliers, colleagues and others.

1 Acting with transparency, honesty, fairness and with discretion

Behaving in an ethical manner involves acting appropriately and therefore with:

- Transparency
- Honesty
- Fairness
- Discretion

We can use these qualities to decide what constitutes appropriate behaviour in any given situation.

Ethical matters often require the use of personal judgement as to the 'right' way to handle them.

Behaviour/ Examples	Description
Transparency	This means presenting information clearly and with not withholding information.
Examples	Prepare financial statements as completely and accurately as possible with clarity.

Behaviour/ Examples	Description
Honesty	This involves being truthful and not trying to mislead or deceive others.
Examples	Taking 'sick days' when you are not sick is dishonest.

Behaviour/ Examples	Description
Fairness	This means treating others equally.
Examples	You must not discriminate against others on a variety of grounds, including race and religious beliefs. Pay should be fair and in line with or above the minimum wage. This shows respect and support for employees.

Behaviour/ Examples	Description
Discretion	This involves being diplomatic and sensitive to other people's rights and feelings.
Examples	Where a person has authority over another person this is particularly important.

Activity 1: Unethical and dishonest behaviour

List some examples of behaviours that would be considered dishonest by you either as a student accountant or an employee. Include an example of dishonest behaviour where the perpetrator may not even be aware it was dishonest.

Activity 2: Behaviour and appropriate action

Shona is a member in business. She has recently employed Harry as a new trainee accountant. Harry regularly checks Facebook during the working day.

Required

Answer the following questions.

(a) What is an appropriate course of action for Shona to take?

	✓
Report him to the AAT.	
Dismiss him.	
Discuss this with him in private and ask him to refrain from logging onto Facebook during working hours.	

(b) If Shona chooses the course of action selected in part a, what behaviour is she demonstrating?

	✓
Integrity	
Discretion	
Honesty	

2 Safeguards to protect against threats to fundamental principles

Members are often involved in the preparation and reporting of information that is used by a wide range of stakeholders.

For example, a company's financial statements may be prepared by the in-house accountants and then used by shareholders.

Members must take reasonable steps to ensure that the financial statements (or other information):

(i)   Describe the true nature of business transactions, assets or liabilities

(ii) Record the information accurately and in a timely manner

(iii) Represent the facts accurately and completely

Assessment focus point

There may be many potential conflicts that make it difficult for the member to perform their work to an appropriate standard. The AAT *Code of Professional Ethics* (2017) refers to them as threats to the fundamental principles. In the assessment always look out for clues on how the fundamental principles can be threatened or compromised.

Activity 3: Five threats to the fundamental ethical principles

Ella is employed as a buyer for a High Street chain of fashion stores trading as Match 'N Clothing. As part of her role Ella has discretion on the suppliers to use and the goods to purchase. Due to the number of stores that Match 'N Patch Clothing have, order quantities and values can be substantial.

Match 'N Patch Clothing has recently has problems in sourcing enough current-trend garments to cover next season's demand. Ella's supervisor, Jake, has mentioned to Ella that if she does not manage to purchase enough goods for the next season then she will be asked to leave the company. The supervisor made it very clear to Ella that she could easily be replaced. Fortunately for Ella, she has an uncle who has an import and export business who has suggested that he would be able to provide Ella with all the goods that she needs to find from overseas. The goods that the Uncle can supply will be last year's styles and would be slightly more expensive than can be purchased from other suppliers. The good news is that Ella's uncle will pay Ella a commission of £0.50 per garment.

Ella has taken up her Uncle's offer and has purchased 1,000 garments from him. Normally, when a supplier sends an invoice to Match 'N Patch Clothing the invoice would be checked by Jake before payment is authorised. However, as this invoice is from a family member, Ella checked the invoice herself and sent it onto the accounts department for payment.

The accounts department has refused to make this payment on the grounds that the invoice has not been properly authorised, and brought this breakdown in process to Jake's attention. When Jake asked Ella why this invoice had been sent to the accounts department without his authorisation, Ella justified this by explaining this was done so that the business could obtain the garments quickly, with the aim of getting them to stores quicker, in time for the new season. Jake was not impressed with this explanation.

Required

To recap, list the five threats to the fundamental principles identified in the AAT *Code of Professional Ethics* (2017: p.11).

Threat

2.1 Accountants in practice and business

Since members who work in an accountancy practice are affected by different threats to those working in a commercial business, most codes make specific recommendations for each situation.

The following tables summarise the main threats to members in practice and business.

Threats: members in practice

Threat category	Specific threats
Self-interest	• Having a financial interest or joint financial interest in a client
	• Depending upon a client's fees for a significant portion of your income
	• Having a close personal relationship with a client
	• Having concerns about losing a client
	• Potential employment with a client
	• Contingent fees (these are fees that depend on the results of the work)
	• Receiving a loan from a client or from its directors or officers
Self-review	• Discovery of a significant error when re-evaluating your work
	• Reporting on the operation of systems after being involved in designing them
	• Preparing the data which is used to generate reports that you are required to check
	• Being, or having recently been, a director or officer of a client you are now auditing or being employed by the client in a position to exert significant influence over the subject matter of the engagement
Familiarity	• Having a close or personal relationship with a director or officer of a client or with an employee of the client who is in a position to exert significant influence over the engagement
	• A former partner of a firm is now employed in a senior position of the client so they are able to exert significant influence on the direction of the work
	• Accepting significant gifts or preferential treatment from a client

Threat category	Specific threats
Intimidation	• Threat of dismissal, replacement, or litigation in respect of an engagement • Pressure to reduce the quality of your work in order to keep fees down • Pressure to agree with the judgement of an employee of the client who has more expertise on a specific matter
Advocacy	• Acting on behalf of a client that is in dispute with a third party

Threats: members in business

Threat category	Specific threats
Self-interest	• Having a financial interest (eg shares or a loan) in the employer • Financial incentives and rewards based on results or profits (including commissions) • Opportunity to use corporate assets to your own advantage • Threats to your job security or promotion prospects • Commercial pressure from outside the organisation
Self-review	• Being asked to review data or justify or evaluate business decisions that you have been involved in preparing or making
Familiarity	• Having a close or personal relationship with someone who may benefit from your influence • Long association with a business contact, which may influence your decisions • Acceptance of a significant gift or preferential treatment, which might be thought to influence your decisions
Intimidation	• Threat of dismissal or replacement over a disagreement over the application of an accounting principle or the manner in which financial information is reported • A dominant individual attempting to influence your decisions
Advocacy	• There is unlikely to be a significant advocacy threat to employees of an organisation. This is because they are entitled and expected to promote the employer's position or viewpoint, as part of furthering its legitimate goals and objectives, though as professional accountants they also have a duty to society (the public interest) as a whole

Illustration 1: Identification of threats

Jane works as a member in practice with Jones and Jones LLP. She is currently engaged on an assurance project for Smith plc. Jane's parents have recently transferred ownership of their 3% shareholding in Smith plc to Jane.

This can be a threat of self-interest as Jane will now have a personal interest on the success of Smith plc. This may risk Jane's objectivity or integrity in completion of the assurance project. Accountants need to be and also seen to be independent so an appropriate safeguard here can be the removal of Jane from the engagement. An alternative option would be for Jane to dispose of the shareholding in Smith plc.

Both of these actions would ensure that the fundamental ethical principles are being adhered to.

Activity 4: Potential threat to fundamental ethical principles

An accountant has been told that they will be subject to disciplinary action unless they interpret an accounting standard in a particular way.

Required

Which one of the following threats is most relevant here?

	✓
Self-review	
Intimidation	
Familiarity	
Advocacy	

Assessment focus point

Always take care when answering written tasks and read task requirements carefully. Is the task asking for ethical principles to be **identified** or is the examiner looking for the **threats** to the ethical principles?

Also, give the number of suggestions asked for. If the task asks for three threats to be suggested then be sure to give three suggestions!

Safeguards

In this section we will consider the safeguards that can be applied to help reduce the risk from any threats identified.

Safeguards are defined as actions that may eliminate threats or reduce them to an acceptable level.

Safeguards fall into two broad categories:

- Safeguards created by the profession, legislation or regulation
- Safeguards in the work environment

Assessment focus point

In the assessment you may have to identify not only the ethical threats but also identify the best course of action, in other words the most appropriate safeguards to reduce or eliminate the threats you have identified.

You need to know about the threats and safeguards relevant to both members in practice and members in business, regardless of your current role.

2.2 Threats and safeguards – members in practice

The *AAT Code of Professional Ethics* (2017) identifies safeguards for members in practice, which can be used in the work environment to protect against threats to the fundamental principles.

They include:

- Leaders in the firm who demonstrate the importance of compliance with the fundamental principles

- Policies and procedures to monitor the quality of engagements, relationships between engagement teams and clients, and revenue received from any one client

- Using different partners or engagements teams for assurance and non-assurance engagements

- Disciplinary procedures to promote compliance with policies

The next activity takes a practical approach to exploring the threats facing members in practice and safeguards that can be put in place to overcome these threats.

Activity 5: Safeguards to reduce threats

Consider the threats facing members in practice. What safeguards should be put in place to eliminate the threat or reduce it to an acceptable level?

Required

Complete the table below.

THREATS	POSSIBLE SAFEGUARDS
Self-interest	
Financial interest in a client (eg owning shares)	
Undue dependence on the client for fee income	
Close business relationship with a client	
Self-review	
Preparing a subject matter (eg financial statements) and then performing assurance work on them (eg an audit)	
A member of the assurance team has recently been employed by the client, and was in a position to exert significant influence over the subject matter	
Advocacy	
Acting as an advocate on behalf of an assurance client in litigation, or disputes with third parties	
Familiarity	
A member of the engagement team having a close relationship with the client	
Accepting gifts from a client	
Long association of senior personnel with the assurance client	

Intimidation	
Being threatened with dismissal on a client engagement	
An assurance client indicating they will not award a planned non-assurance contract if the member in practice disagrees with the client on an issue	
Being threatened with litigation	

2.3 Threats and safeguards – members in business

In this section we will consider safeguards for members in business, which can be used to protect against threats to the fundamental principles.

Examples include:

- Recruitment procedures (employ high calibre staff)
- Strong internal controls
- Appropriate disciplinary processes
- Monitoring employee performance
- Communicating policies and procedures to all employees
- Leadership which stresses the importance of ethical behaviour
- Policies and procedures to encourage employees to communicate to senior personnel on any ethical issues which concern them

Activity 6: Fundamental ethical principles threatened in business

You are a professional accountant working in business. A colleague has told you that one of the directors has offered him a sum of money to manipulate next quarter's VAT return. When your colleague refused to cooperate the director became angry and abusive.

Required

Explain how the fundamental ethical principles could be threatened here

Activity 7: Safeguards in business

Required

Answer the following question by selecting the appropriate option.

A business's authorisation policy states that purchase requisitions over £100 must be signed by two different employees.

This part of the policy is primarily designed to

▼

.

Picklist:

ensure the purchase process operates more quickly
encourage employees to communicate with each other
reduce the risk of employees misappropriating business assets

3 The accountant and client relationship

Acting with integrity, honesty and fairness does not just apply to performance in the work of the accountant. There are a number of matters relating to relationships with clients that are relevant to members in practice.

Professional appointment and transfer of clients

For all sorts of reasons, a client may wish to change from one professional adviser to another. They may be relocating, or looking for a more (or different) specialised expertise – or lower fees.

Where a client is looking to switch advisers, the key ethical issue is how to protect the interests of all parties, by ensuring that information that is relevant to the change of appointment is properly exchanged.

An important point to bear in mind when accepting a new appointment is to ensure that doing so does not breach any of the fundamental principles and whether there are any threats arising from the appointment.

Money laundering prevention and customer due diligence

When acquiring clients, and also when working with continuing clients, the accountant must always be aware of the risk that their services are being used to facilitate **money laundering or terrorist financing**. The applicable anti-money laundering legislation in the UK consists of:

- **The Proceeds of Crime Act 2002** (as amended)

- **The Terrorism Act 2000** (as amended)

- **The Money Laundering, Terrorist Financing and Transfer of Funds (Information on the Payer) Regulations 2017** (as amended)

The AAT will also expect members to carry out **customer due diligence** on clients, report money laundering or terrorist financing, and keep proper records. Failure to comply with these requirements results in a breach of professional behaviour.

Assessment focus point

Customer due diligence is a process undertaken before accepting a new assignment to identify any threats or risks to the fundamental principles. In the assessment you may need to identify whether due diligence is needed by looking out for any unusual circumstances with the new assignment.

Customer due diligence provisions of the **Money Laundering Regulations 2017** will apply in certain circumstances and when the relevant monetary threshold for a related occasional transaction (or series of transactions) is exceeded.

The regulations (TSO, 2017) state that customer due diligence **must** be applied when:

- A member enters a professional relationship with a client which will have an element of duration

- The member acts in relation to a transaction or series of related transactions amounting to, or more than, €15,000 (or the equivalent in sterling)

- There is a suspicion of money laundering or terrorist financing

- Where there are doubts about previously obtained customer identification

- At appropriate times to existing clients on a risk-sensitive basis

The client's identity must be verified on the basis of documents or other reliable information.

Customer due diligence must be carried out on all **new** clients **before** providing any services to them. The **one exception** to this rule is where undertaking customer due diligence would interrupt the normal conduct of business and the risk of money laundering and terrorist financing is very low.

For **new clients**, customer due diligence will start with finding out who the client claims to be and obtaining the evidence to substantiate this.

Activity 8: New client relationship

When accepting a new client relationship an accountant in practice must consider:

	✓
How profitable the relationship will be	
Whether acceptance would create any threats to compliance with the fundamental principles	
Whether the client's directors meet the firm's moral and ethical standards	

Activity 9: Customer due diligence – true or false

Hubert, a member in practice, wishes to enter into a professional relationship with a client which is expected to last for at least two years.

Required

(a) Explain whether the following statements are true or false.

Statement	Explanation
Hubert can verify the client's identity through an informal discussion with the chief accountant.	
If due diligence is not possible Hubert can still perform professional services for this client for two years.	

(b) As part of his customer due diligence processes, which of the following actions must Hubert take?

Statement	✓
Notify the police of the relationship	
Verify the client's identity on the basis of documents, data or other reliable information	
Verify the nature and value of the client's assets	

For **existing clients**, ongoing monitoring must be undertaken. This involves carrying out appropriate customer due diligence procedures on any transactions that appear inconsistent with existing knowledge of the client, and keeping customer due diligence records up to date.

Activity 10: Customer due diligence and existing clients

Bill and Ben Ltd, a small engineering company, has unexpectedly requested your practice to help in a gambling licence application and assistance in looking for a nightclub with a cost up to £10 million.

Required

Explain whether customer due diligence should be carried before accepting this work.

3.1 Recommendations, referrals and commissions

A satisfied client may introduce others to your practice, and that's fine. You might also offer a **commission**, fee or reward to your employees for bringing in a new client. But you should never offer financial incentives to a third party to introduce clients (a referral fee or commission) – unless:

- The client is aware that the third party has been paid for the referral
- The third party is also bound by professional (or comparable) ethical standards, and can be trusted to carry out the introduction with integrity

Accountants might also pay a **referral fee** to obtain a client. This could arise in the situation where the client continues as a client of another firm but requires specialist services not offered by that firm.

3.2 Constraints on services to be supplied

The main constraint on the services that an accountant provides is that they should not take on work they are not competent to perform. This is to protect against breaching the principle of professional competence and due care.

It is important to note that there are certain services that an accountant cannot legally offer unless they are **authorised** to do so by the **relevant regulatory body** in the UK. These services, known as **'reserved areas'** are:

- **External audit** of UK limited companies, or where the services of a registered auditor are required
- **Investment business** (including agency for a building society) and the provision of corporate financial advice
- **Insolvency practice** (company liquidations and administration)

3.3 Conflicts of interest

Conflicts can arise between an accountant and their client due to a number of circumstances and preventing conflicts is key to ensuring a professional distance is maintained between the accountant and client.

Examples of conflicts include when a firm undertakes services for clients whose interests are in conflict or where clients are in dispute with each other.

If the threat is **significant** then the accountant should consider whether it is ethical to continue with one or any of the appointments.

If the threat is **not clearly significant** then there are safeguards that can be put in place. These safeguards can include:

- Using separate engagement teams and **Chinese walls** between teams

- Creating different areas of practice within the firm that prevent the passing of confidential information

- Having procedures in place to prevent access to information

- Regular reviews of the application of safeguards by a senior person not involved with those engagements

- Have key judgements and conclusions reviewed by a professional accountant not connected with the service

- Restructuring responsibilities and duties

- Have work supervised by a non-executive director

- Withdraw from decision-making where a conflict exists

- Consult third parties such as professional bodies, accountants and legal counsel

The above safeguards essentially mean that when you accept a new appointment, or become aware of changes in the circumstances of an existing client, you should check whether this might create a conflict of interest with another client. **The general principle is that the interests of one client must not have a negative effect on the interests of another.**

Activity 11: Conflict of interest and two clients

A firm of accountants has two clients that are in the same business and compete against each other.

Explain how this could result in a conflict of interest and suggest safeguards that can be put in place to reduce or eliminate this risk.

3.4 Second opinions

In some instances, a client of another firm may seek your opinion on the advice they have received from that firm. This is known as a **second opinion**. When dealing with a request for a second opinion, the accountant should evaluate the significance of any threats and apply appropriate safeguards if the threats are significant.

Appropriate safeguards could include:

- Seeking the client's permission to contact the existing accountant
- Describing the limitations surrounding any opinion in communications with the client
- Providing the existing accountant with a copy of the opinion

3.5 Fees and other types of remuneration

When entering into negotiations regarding professional services, a member in practice may quote whatever fee is deemed to be appropriate.

Accountants often provide services for clients in return for fees which are charged on a time basis. This means the actual charge to their client will be based on:

> **Length of time spent on the engagement multiplied by charge-out rate.**

The charge-out rate is usually expressed as an hourly rate, which will vary depending on the level and experience of staff.

3.6 Ethical considerations

The AAT *Code of Professional Ethics* observes that if the fee quoted is too low it may be difficult to perform the engagement in accordance with the relevant technical and professional standards.

When determining the fee, accountants must:

- Make the client aware of the terms of the engagement
- Explain the basis on which fees are charged
- Explain which services are covered by the quoted fee
- Assign appropriate time and staff to the task

Activity 12: Low fees

Hugh, an AAT member in practice, is keen to continue providing services for Amelia Ltd. He is considering charging them a fee which is low in relation to the amount of time he will spend on the engagement, and his hourly charge-out rate.

What type of threat does this give rise to and which fundamental principle is threatened?

Required

Select your answers from the drag items below and include them in the table provided.

Ethical threat	Fundamental principle

Drag items:

Advocacy	Familiarity	Intimidation	Self-interest	Self-review
Confidentiality	Integrity	Objectivity	Professional behaviour	Professional competence and due care

3.7 Contingent fees

A contingent fee is a fee calculated on a predetermined basis relating to the outcome of a transaction or the result of the work performed. Contingent fees are used widely for certain types of non-assurance engagements, for example debt recovery work.

There is a risk that they give rise to threats to compliance with the fundamental principles. Therefore, they are not used for assurance engagements.

3.8 Out-of-pocket expenses

Out-of-pocket expenses that are directly related to the work performed for a particular client (such as travelling expenses) may be charged to the client for reimbursement, in addition to professional fees.

Illustration 2: Fees and out-of-pocket expenses

You have just had a phone call from a prospective new client, asking about fees. You offer a free-of-charge consultation to discuss the matter. The client has recently left his job to become a freelance photographer; in the first instance, he requires an accountant to prepare financial statements and tax returns, and to advise on financial management. The photographer has a number of questions for you.

(1) 'How much will you charge per year?'

(2) 'Do you reduce the fee if you don't save me as much tax as you thought?'

(3) 'What about if I get you to help me with a proposal for an Arts Grant that's available for photographers, will you accept a commission on that, instead of an hourly rate?'

(4) 'What about expenses and will I be paying for all this nice office space?'

Appropriate responses to the new client:

(1) Fees are based on an hourly rate based on the complexity of the work.

(2) A contingent fee cannot be set on this basis, nor can you make any promises in relation to tax savings

(3) This could be possible, to work on a commission basis.

(4) No, this is covered in overall charge-out rates and clients will only be charged out-of-pocket expenses directly related to work completed.

3.9 Marketing professional services

To attract new clients, accountancy practices may advertise their services to the public and businesses. As in any form of advertising there are risks of misrepresenting your services and of making claims that damage the competition, either deliberately or negligently. In other words how a practice advertises itself, and how it tries to win an advantage over its competitors, is an ethical issue.

Accountants must not bring the profession into **disrepute** when marketing their services. This includes being **honest and truthful** and not making **exaggerated claims** for the services offered, qualifications or experience, and not making **disparaging references or unsubstantiated comparisons** to the work of others.

The general principle is that a professional practice, and its individual accountants, need to:

- Project an image consistent with the 'dignity' (the high ethical and technical standards) of the profession

- Maintain integrity in all promotional actions and statements

Aggressive following up of contacts and leads is considered good marketing in some contexts – but it can be both counter-productive (by putting clients off) and unethical if you are promoting professional services. If you contact or approach potential clients directly and repeatedly, or otherwise in a 'pushy' manner, you may be open to a complaint of harassment.

If fees are used as a promotional tool, the fee should not lead to reduced quality of the work undertaken. Although the offering of 'free' services should be avoided, a **free initial consultation** is considered ethically sound.

Activity 13: Conflict of interest and fees

You are an accountant in practice and while advising a software developer called Jose, he mentions that he used to receive financial advice from a small firm of accountants in the centre of the neighbouring town.

Jose tells you they had very low advertised rates, offered a free initial consultation, and often claimed that they were 'the best accountancy practice in the region'.

Required

(a) **Answer the following questions by selecting the appropriate options.**

Questions	Solutions
Could it be misleading to refer to your accountancy practice as the 'best in the region'?	▼
Why is this the case?	▼

Picklist:

'Best' is ambiguous and difficult to prove
'Best' accurately describes how the accountancy firm compares to its competitors
No
Yes

(b) **Indicate whether the statements are true or false by selecting the appropriate option.**

Description	True ✓	False ✓
If the fees are set too low, this may result in a reduction in the quality of the work undertaken.		
It is unethical to offer a free initial consultation.		
Other accountancy services should not be offered for free as the quality of work may be compromised if accountants receive no fee or a reduced fee.		

Chapter summary

- **Behaving ethically** means acting with integrity, honesty, fairness and sensitivity in dealings with clients, suppliers, colleagues and others.

- Accountants face numerous **threats** against the five fundamental ethical principles. These threats can be classified as self-interest, self-review, familiarity, intimidation and advocacy.

- There are a number of **safeguards** against the threats accountants face. Some are described in the ethical code, other sources of safeguards include the law and policies and procedures set out by their employer.

- There are a number of important principles and procedures to follow when an accountant in practice **acquires new clients**. At all times the law must be followed, and respect and dignity should be shown to competitors and the accounting profession. In particular, rules cover:

  - Constraints on the services that can be provided
  - Dealing with conflicts of interest
  - Transferring clients
  - Money laundering regulations
  - Fees and receiving commission for recommending new clients
  - Giving second opinions
  - Marketing professional services

Keywords

- **Chinese walls:** Separate teams working on different clients to reduce any potential conflicts

- **Conflict of interest:** Where there can be disputes or a clash of interests

- **Contingent fees:** A fee calculated on the basis of the outcome of a transaction

- **Customer due diligence:** A process undertaken on new or existing clients to identify any ethical issues before providing services

- **Money Laundering Regulations 2017:** Legislation and obligations surrounding crimes in dealing in, taking part in or using criminal property

- **Referral fees:** A fee received from a third party to obtain a client

- **Reserved areas:** Services that can only be offered when authorised such as external audit, investment business and insolvency practice

- **Safeguards:** Processes aimed to reduce or eliminate any ethical threats

- **Second opinions:** Where a client seeks a further opinion from another firm

Test your learning

1   The discovery of a significant error while re-evaluating your work will give rise to a self-interest threat.

	✓
True	
False	

2   Accepting payment for introducing a client to another firm can give rise to which of the following threats to the fundamental ethical principles?

	✓
Self-interest	
Self-review	
Advocacy	
Familiarity	
Intimidation	

3   Which of these represents a threat to professional competence and due care?

	✓
Providing a second opinion	
Accepting a gift from a supplier	

4   Which Act forms part of UK anti-money laundering legislation?

	✓
The Bribery Act 2010	
The Terrorism Act 2000	

5   What is meant by due diligence?

	✓
A process undertaken before taking on a new engagement to identify any potential threats to the fundamental principles	
Keeping up to date in knowledge and skills and ensuring work is completed with accuracy	

Behaving in an ethical manner – part II

3

Learning outcomes

2.2	**Explain the importance of acting with integrity** Students need to know: • The meaning of integrity from the ethical code • The effect of accountants being associated with misleading information • The meaning of the key ethical values of honesty, transparency and fairness • The importance of acting at all times with integrity, honesty, transparency and fairness when liaising with clients, suppliers and colleagues • How integrity is threatened in particular by self-interest and familiarity threats
2.3	**Explain the importance of objectivity** Students need to know: • What is meant by a conflict of interest, including self-interest threats arising from financial interests, compensation and incentives linked to financial reporting and decision making • How accountants may deal with offers of gifts and hospitality • How gifts and hospitality may pose threats to objectivity as inducements • The link between compromised objectivity and possible accusations of bribery or fraud
2.5	**Explain the importance of being competent and acting with due care** Students need to know: • How professional qualifications and continuing professional development (CPD) support professional competence • The areas in which up-to-date technical knowledge for an accountant's competence may be critical • The consequences of an accountant failing to work competently and with due care • The link between lack of professional competence or due care and: claims for breach of contract in the supply of services and professional negligence; accusations of fraud or money laundering

2.6	Explain the importance of confidentiality and when confidential information may be disclosed
	Students need to know:
	• When it may be appropriate to disclose confidential information
	• When confidential information must be disclosed
	• To whom a disclosure of confidential information may be made
	• How information confidentiality may be affected by compliance with data protection laws
3.4	Justify an appropriate action when requested to perform tasks that are beyond current experience of expertise
	Students need to be able to:
	• Recognise in a given situation that an accountant has been asked to complete work for which they do not have sufficient expertise, information, time, training or resources
	• Decide the appropriate time at which advice about such concerns should be sought
	• Decide what to do in such a situation

Assessment context

You will be asked to demonstrate your knowledge of how to behave in an ethical manner when working with internal and external clients while in practice. There are a number of threats and safeguards linked specifically to client-based work and you must understand the role you play in maintaining the integrity of the profession.

Qualification context

Whether you work in practice or business it is important that you understand all of the rules, codes, regulations and legislation for your future career as an AAT member.

Business context

Accountants are given a significant amount of responsibility. The integrity of the practice you work for is at stake if you choose the wrong course of action. In a client facing role you must recognise the principles the AAT *Code of Professional Ethics* is based on and to the best of your ability put safeguards in place to protect yourself and those you work with.

Chapter overview

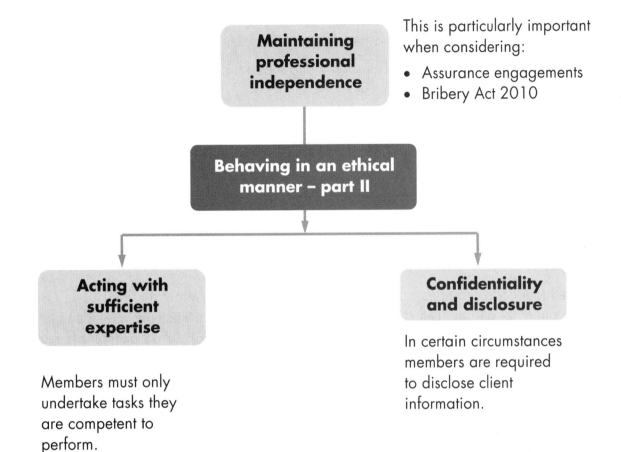

Maintaining professional independence

This is particularly important when considering:

- Assurance engagements
- Bribery Act 2010

Behaving in an ethical manner – part II

Acting with sufficient expertise

Members must only undertake tasks they are competent to perform.

This is necessary to comply with the fundamental principle of professional competence and due care.

Confidentiality and disclosure

In certain circumstances members are required to disclose client information.

Introduction

An accountant has a duty to maintain an appropriate **professional distance** between their work and their personal life at all times. This is required in order to be able act objectively, ie independence and objectivity are linked.

In this chapter we will look at various specific situations that may be encountered both by members in practice and members in business:

- Maintaining professional objectivity and independence
- Acting with sufficient expertise
- Confidentiality and disclosure

1 Objectivity and professional independence

The fundamental principle of objectivity requires accountants not to compromise their **professional judgement** due to bias, conflict of interest or undue influence or other reasons.

It is important that members are not only independent but also seen to be independent by others.

The ethical code provides advice on how accountants can maintain their objectivity in relation to all services. Where significant threats to objectivity are identified, safeguards have to be applied to eliminate or reduce threats to an acceptable level (if you are unsure of potential threats that can exist please refer back to the previous chapter). Safeguards to threats can include the following:

- Withdrawing from the engagement team
- Supervisory procedures
- Terminating the financial or business arrangement
- Discussions with the senior management of the firm
- Discussions with those charged with governance at the client

If there are no safeguards that can eliminate or reduce the threat to an acceptable level, the engagement must be declined or terminated.

There are specific situations or threats associated with lack of professional distance between professional duties and personal life due to lack of independence. These can be relevant to members both in business and in practice.

For members in practice, being independent is particularly important for those involved in assurance engagements such as external audits.

Statutory audits are an example of an assurance engagement and demonstrate the importance of members in practice maintaining professional independence while acting for a client.

As one of the duties of a professional accountant can be the preparation of financial statements it worth looking at how this duty fits in with the performance of a company, the parties involved and whether there is any incentive to manipulate results. These aspects are covered in the activity below:

Activity 1: Financial statements and performance

Required

Answer the questions below to complete the table.

Question	Solution
How do we know how a company has performed over the year?	
Who is responsible for preparing the financial statements?	
Do they have an incentive to manipulate the figures?	
How do we measure whether the financial statements are reasonable?	
Who are the primary users of the financial statements?	
How do they know they can rely on the financial statements?	

The AAT *Code* (2017) defines an assurance engagement as an engagement:

'in which a member in practice expresses a conclusion designed to enhance the degrees of confidence of the intended users other than the responsible party about the outcome of the evaluation of a subject matter against criteria' (p.52).

The key terms are:

Terms	Example – using an audit engagement
Subject matter	Financial statements
Criteria	(International) Financial Reporting Standards
Practitioner	Members in practice
Responsible party	Company directors
Intended users	Shareholders

Members in practice must be independent of their assurance clients. This is required so that they can act objectively and provide an independent opinion on the financial statements.

What does the AAT *Code* mean by independence?

Independence in mind means a state of mind that permits an individual to act with integrity, objectivity and professional scepticism.

Independence in appearance is where a third party would consider the member's integrity, objectivity and professional scepticism has not been compromised.

This is consistent with the principles-based approach. The AAT *Code* (2017) advises a **conceptual approach** to independence rather than adherence to rigid rules.

Audit committee

An audit committee is a sub-committee of the board of directors, made up of non-executive directors. At least one member of the audit committee should have relevant financial experience.

Their duties include the following:

- Recommending the appointment, reappointment and removal of the external auditors to shareholders

- Monitoring the external auditors' independence

- Monitoring the supply of non-audit services by the external audit firm.

Financial interests

There are a number of ways in which an accountant in business could gain financially from their activities for an employer – and many of these might pose a self-interest threat to the fundamental ethical principles such as integrity, confidentiality, or objectivity.

An example of a financial interest is where an employee may have shares in their employing company so will have a direct interest in the financial results of the company.

Illustration 1: A financial interest threat

A senior member of staff is eligible for a sales-related bonus based on sales revenue generated. This can be seen as a significant threat to this staff member's independence and objectivity as the decisions of this individual can impact on the value of the bonus received. For example, selling goods at an unprofitable price in order to increase sales revenue.

Once this threat has been identified safeguards need to be put in place to eliminate or reduce this threat. Possible safeguards can be discussed through a remuneration committee or officers charged with corporate governance in addition to consulting with external professional bodies for guidance.

One potential safeguard could be changing the bonus system to profit based rather than sales based.

1.1 Gifts, hospitality and inducements

One of the key threats to independence and objectivity is the accepting of gifts, services, favours or hospitality from parties who may have an interest in the outcome of the accountant's work.

Parties here can include:

- A work colleague
- A client if working in practice
- Any party with a current or proposed contractual relationship with an employing organisation, for example contractors and suppliers.

Gifts, hospitality or inducements may be (or may be seen to be) an attempt to influence the objectivity of an accountant's decisions. While not actually influenced there is an issue of a wider public perception as accountants must be seen to be above suspicion of being influenced.

Does this mean that an individual cannot accept bottle of wine at Christmas, or a calendar from a supplier? No. The gift needs to be significant enough to be reasonably perceived by a third party to influence judgement.

Activity 2: Gifts, hospitality and inducements

Harry is a member in practice. His client, Silver Ltd owns a large chain of pizza restaurants. Silver Ltd has recently merged with another pizza chain, so business is likely to grow significantly in the coming year.

To celebrate, Silver Ltd offers Harry and all the company's other suppliers a gift voucher for use in one of the restaurants, to the value of £25.

Required

Should Harry accept the gift?

	✓
Yes – members in practice are entitled to receive any gift offered by a client, regardless of the value of the gift.	
Yes – the offer is made to Harry and all other suppliers, and the gift is not significant enough to influence his judgement.	
No – the gift is significant, and could be perceived as likely to influence his judgement.	

As part of the conceptual framework approach, the AAT *Code* (2017) gives the following advice: If a reasonable and informed third party, having knowledge of all relevant information, would consider the inducement insignificant then the member may conclude that the offer is made in the normal course of business and generally conclude there is no significant threat.

Possible safeguards to eliminate or reduce related significant threats to an acceptable level include the following:

- Informing senior management
- Informing third parties such as a professional body
- Advising close or personal relations of any potential threats

Activity 3: Independence in practice

A member in practice on an assurance engagement must be independent of their client.

Required

(a) Which one option best indicates what independence means to an AAT member in practice?

	✓
Independence in mind	
Independence in appearance	
Independence in both mind and appearance	

(b) Indicate whether the statement is true or false by selecting the appropriate option.

Description	True ✓	False ✓
Members in practice must demonstrate they are independent of assurance clients by applying a rigid set of rules.		
Members in practice must demonstrate they are independent of assurance clients by taking a conceptual framework approach to independence.		

1.2 The Bribery Act 2010

How to deal with gifts, hospitality and inducements has long been an issue as it can sometimes be difficult to draw a line between legally developing and maintaining mutual business relationships and actual criminal acts of bribery and corruption.

Bribery occurs when a person offers or promises a financial or other advantage to another individual in exchange for improperly performing a function or activity.

The Bribery Act 2010 is UK legislation that came into force in 2011 and applies to both individuals and organisations. The Act makes giving, receiving or offering bribes a criminal offence.

The Bribery Act 2010 (Ministry of Justice, 2010) introduces four offences to UK law:

- Bribing another person
- Being bribed
- Bribing a foreign official
- Failure of a commercial organisation to prevent bribery

The penalties imposed if individuals or companies are found guilty of bribery are severe. Individuals may be imprisoned for up to **10 years** and face an **unlimited fine**. Companies may face an unlimited fine along with bad publicity and loss of reputation.

Activity 4: Factors to consider when accepting hospitality

You have been recently employed as a payables ledger clerk for a construction company. Your manager has been granted ten tickets to attend the Ashes test match at Lord's Cricket Ground, London, in a corporate hospitality box by a consultancy firm that is bidding for the contract to design your company's new computer system.

Required

Describe the factors that will determine whether there is an ethical issue arising from the granting of the tickets.

Activity 5: Identifying bribes

Explain if any of the following scenarios would constitute an offence under the Bribery Act 2010.

Scenario	Explanation
You meet an old friend in a bar who works for another audit firm. During your chat she offers to buy you another drink if you would explain how a spreadsheet formula could be used in her audit work.	
You are an accounting technician working in practice and a senior partner from another accountancy firm telephones you and offers you a seat in a box at a Premier League football match. You wasn't sure at the time as the line was bad but the partner also mentioned something about a client list.	
Your team has been working long hours to ensure a deadline is met for the submission of a client's financial statements. The financial statements were submitted with a day to spare. The client admits that it was his bad record keeping that caused this delayed submission and as a thank you insists on taking the whole team out for a chicken meal. As your team has twenty members this could be expensive for the client.	

Scenario	Explanation
One of your clients is in the process of applying for a large bank loan. Although, you have only known the client for a month the client has asked you to supply a reference to the bank stating that you have known her for three years. The client has mentioned she has a luxury apartment in Spain that she normally lets out to holidaymakers but you are welcome to use this free of charge during August.	

2 Acting with sufficient expertise

We now look at the issue of acting with sufficient expertise.

Members must only undertake tasks that they are competent to perform, or where they have access to the necessary supervision or training which enables them to perform those tasks competently.

This is necessary to comply with the fundamental principle of **professional competence and due care**. Due care means that having agreed to do a task you have an obligation to carry it out to the best of your ability.

Members must not intentionally mislead an employer as to their level of expertise. They must seek appropriate expert advice when required.

Threats to professional competence and due care are:

- Insufficient time to spend on duties
- Inadequate information for performing the duties properly
- Insufficient experience or training
- Inadequate resources

Safeguards should be put in place to eliminate the threats or reduce them to an acceptable level.

Safeguards can include the following:

- Obtaining additional advice or training
- Ensuring there is enough time for the work to be completed
- Getting help from someone with the relevant knowledge
- Consulting with a supervisor or the relevant professional body

If the threat cannot be eliminated or reduced to an acceptable level, the member must refuse to perform the duties.

Assessment focus point

When there are issues of sufficient expertise this will be normally associated with a breach of the ethical principle of professional competence and due care. One of the ways of maintaining both sufficient expertise and professional competence is the completion of regular continuing professional development (CPD).

Activity 6: Safeguards to reduce threats

Members must be aware of any potential threats to the fundamental ethical principle of professional competence and due care.

Required

Identify the safeguards that can be put in place to eliminate or reduce them to an acceptable level.

Threats	Possible safeguard
Insufficient time to spend on duties	
Inadequate information to perform the duties properly	
Insufficient experience or knowledge	
Inadequate resources	

Assessment focus point

In your assessment you may need to suggest possible safeguards to put in place to safeguard against threats to the ethical principles. Many times safeguards will be unable to eliminate a threat 100% so merely bringing risks down to an **acceptable level** will be satisfactory.

If an assignment is not completed with due care then this can result in a **breach of contract** through **professional negligence.** This means a failure to act with due skill and care, causing loss to another party and there may be a liability to pay the injured party compensation.

Accountants are in a **position of trust** with their clients because they hold sensitive information relating to them and hold a degree of power in the relationship, being an expert in their field.

This position of trust may be broken if the accountant fails to act in the best interests of the client.

To safeguard against the risk of being found liable to pay compensation, accountants may add a **disclaimer of liability** to their work. This is a statement that says the author of the work will not be responsible for any loss suffered by someone who acts upon the work completed.

The effectiveness of such disclaimers is open to question by a court and such a statement is unlikely to protect a member who has not acted with due care.

Activity 7: Inadequate information and consequences

Marcy, a professional accountant in practice has knowingly prepared a set of financial statements for Dan on the basis of inadequate information.

Required

Answer the questions below regarding the above scenario

	Explanation
Which of the fundamental principles are most threatened here?	
If Dan receives a fine due to these financial statements, on what grounds could Dan receive compensation from Marcy?	

UK Fraud Act 2006

Under the UK Fraud Act 2006 (TSO, 2006) a person is guilty of fraud if they are in breach of any of the following offences:

- Fraud by false representation
- Fraud by failing to disclose information
- Fraud by abuse of position

Fraud by false representation

For example, an accountant in business may be tempted to understate their company's liabilities (eg loans) to make the company appear more attractive to a potential investor.

Fraud by failing to disclose information

We will discuss fraud by failing to disclose information in the next section when we consider money laundering.

Fraud by abuse of position

Professional accountants may need to hold client money in order to perform their professional duties. For example, they may have custody over a client's bank account so that they can manage their client's financial affairs, perhaps while their client is overseas.

Therefore, the accountant **could** be tempted to commit fraud and use the client's money to benefit themselves.

The maximum penalties under the UK Fraud Act 2006 are 10 years' imprisonment and an unlimited fine.

Activity 8: Types of fraud

Julia is a member in practice. Pickering is a landlord with 10 properties, which he rents to other businesses. Six months ago he transferred £20,000 to Julia to be used for repairs and other expenses that may be needed to maintain his properties while he is overseas.

Pickering has returned to the UK and is surprised when Julia informs him she now only holds £1,000 of his money.

Required

Under the UK Fraud Act 2006, which is the most likely offence Julia has committed?

Type of offence	✓
Fraud by false representation	
Fraud by failing to disclose information	
Fraud by abuse of position	

Handling client monies

Accountants who work in practice may come into contact with client monies. **Client monies** are any funds, or other documents that can be converted into money that the accountant in practice holds on behalf of a client.

This does not include the member in practice's fees due or held by the practice.

Handling clients' money – key safeguards and conditions

Holding client money can result in self-interest threats to integrity, objectivity and professional behaviour. The following are safeguards related to **separation, use** and **accountability.**

- **Separation** – Clients' money must be kept separate from the money belonging to the accountant personally or to the practice.

- **Use** – Clients' money must only be used for the purpose intended.

- **Accountability** – Accountants must be ready at all times to account for the money, ie adequate record keeping and availability to return to the client when requested.

Accountants in practice should not hold clients' monies if:

- They are the monies of investment business clients and the accountant is not regulated

- There is a reason to believe the money is 'criminal property'

- There is no justification in holding the money

- There is a condition on the accountant's licence or registration to prohibit dealing in client monies

3 Confidentiality and disclosure

Members have access to sensitive information about their clients, and it is important that clients and prospective clients can trust their accountant to treat it with great care.

The principle of confidentiality means that members must not:

- As a **general rule**, disclose information about their client's affairs
- Use confidential information acquired through their work to their advantage

The principle of confidentiality continues even after the end of the relationship with a client or employer. The AAT *Code* (2017) explains that members are entitled to use prior experience, when they change employment/acquire a new client, provided they do not disclosure confidential information.

Employers have a responsibility to ensure their staff respect the principle of confidentiality. Many accounting firms issue **confidentiality contracts and guidelines** to all members of staff as a safeguard to protect client confidentiality.

Examples include:

- Information shared with the expectation that it will be kept private and confidential
- Information that is restricted or classified eg marked 'confidential' or 'private'
- Information protected by data protection legislation
- Information that could be used against the interests of an organisation or individual

Disclosure of confidential information

Under the AAT *Code of Professional Ethics* (2017) there are certain circumstances in which members are permitted or required to disclose confidential information.

Circumstances	Examples
Disclosure is permitted by law and authorised by the client or employer	• Disclosure to potential buyers of the client company • Voluntary disclosure to a regulator
Disclosure is required by law and a legal duty to disclose	• Required by legal proceedings • Required by public authorities (eg HMRC) • Actual or suspected money laundering/terrorist financing
Professional duty or right to disclose which is in the public interest and not prohibited by law	• Compliance with IFAC or another professional body • Protection of a member's professional interests in legal proceedings

The AAT *Code* acknowledges that this is a complex area and, where concerns exist, members are advised to seek legal advice.

Non-compliance with laws and regulations

The AAT *Code* gives guidance about what should be done in the situation where a professional accountant encounters non-compliance with laws and regulations – specifically, laws and regulations that either directly affect the financial statements, or which are fundamental to the client's business (AAT *Code*: para. 360.5).

If this happens, then their objectives are:

- To comply with the fundamental principles of integrity and professional behaviour

- By alerting management, to enable them to rectify consequences of the identified or suspected non-compliance, and to deter future non-compliance.

- To take such further action as may be needed in the public interest.

(AAT *Code*: para. 360.4)

The accountant must first obtain an understanding of the non-compliance. The next step is to discuss the matter with the accountant's immediate superior. A response should be made – broadly speaking, to make good the situation and to deter future non-compliance. Once this has been done, it may be necessary to take further action (such as reporting the non-compliance to the relevant authorities) (AAT *Code*: paras. 360. 14-27).

Activity 9: Duty of confidentiality and disclosure

Amir is a professional accountant in practice. He has several pieces of confidential information about one his clients, Derek.

Required

State whether it may be appropriate for Amir to disclose the information in the following circumstances.

Questions	Yes or No
Disclosure if Derek has broken criminal laws	
Disclosure that is not required by law but which is authorised by Derek	

Activity 10: Duty of confidentiality and disclosure

Thomas is an AAT member in practice. One of his clients is being investigated by HMRC. HMRC ask Thomas to provide them with certain information, to assist with their enquiry. Thomas refuses to co-operate saying this would be a breach of his duty of confidentiality to his client.

Required

Answer the questions below by selecting the appropriate answers from the picklist.

Questions	Solution
In what circumstances is Thomas under an obligation to disclose information about his client?	▼
If disclosure is required by law and Thomas refuses to co-operate, is he committing a criminal offence?	▼

Picklist:

Disclosure is authorised by the client
Disclosure is in the public interest
Disclosure is required by law
No
Yes

Data Protection Act 2018

The Data Protection Act 2018 aims to give individuals control over their personal information. It also extends domestic data protection laws to areas which are not covered by Europe-wide data protection legislation, such as the GDPR.

Under the Data Protection Act:

- Anyone who processes personal information must ensure it is protected - business processes handling personal data should be built with privacy by default, and should store the data anonymously (eg using pseudonymisation)

- Individuals have the right to access both their personal data and information about how it is being processed

- Personal data can only be held if there is a specific lawful reason to do so, or if the individual has explicitly opted-in to allow storage of data

Any organisation collecting or holding information about an individual, or using, disclosing, retaining or destroying this information is required to apply the principles of the Data Protection Act.

Every organisation that processes personal information must notify the **Information Commissioner's Office (ICO).** Notification is effective for one year.

Within each organisation or practice there will usually be a person who has the responsibility of informing the ICO of ongoing processing or any changes. This is the role of the **data controller**.

Failure to notify the ICO is a criminal offence.

Here is a useful web address outlining ICO requirements: ico.org.uk

Activity 11: Duty of confidentiality and disclosure

Martin is an AAT member. He has set up a small business with six employees.

Required

Answer the questions below by selecting the appropriate answers from the picklist.

Question	Solution	
Should Martin register with the Information Commissioner?		▼
The reason for this is that Martin		▼

Picklist:

Does not hold personal information
Holds personal information
No
Yes

Activity 12: Disclose or not to disclose

Jane is a qualified accountant in business employed by a city hotel. Jane's responsibilities include maintaining records of daily income from room bookings and also completion a of a quarterly VAT return.

The following information is relevant to Jane's role.

(1) During a routine HMRC visit it was discovered that the hotel owner had been using invoices related to his own personal expenditure to claim for input VAT. Jane was unaware that the expenditure was not valid to reclaim VAT however HMRC are now asking Jane for further information regarding these invoices.

(2) Jane has noted a designated fire exit in the kitchen is continually being blocked by food deliveries. Although Jane has raised this with the head chef and the hotel's owner nothing has been done to resolve this issue. A trading officer is due to visit next Monday to conduct a regular yearly health and safety assessment of the hotel's policies and procedures.

(3) An email has been received by Jane for the attention of 'The accountant'. The email is from an internet website providing reviews of hotels and bed and breakfast establishments. The content of the email requests for Jane to supply the monetary value of room bookings for last year. This information will be displayed on the website along with other hotels in the same city.

Required

Explain how Jane can and should proceed in the above three scenarios.

Chapter summary

- An accountant has a professional duty to maintain an **appropriate professional distance** (independence) between their work and their personal life at all times.

- There is a self-interest threat if members in business, or their close or personal relations or associates have a **financial interest** in their employing organisation.

- **Gifts and hospitality** or **inducements** can also pose self-interest and intimidation threats to an accountant's objectivity and confidentiality.

- Potential threats to the principle of **competence and due care** include: time pressure (when there may not be enough time to complete a task properly); insufficient or inaccurate information; lack of resources (eg equipment or help); or your own lack of experience, knowledge or training.

- Accountants in practice face a number of consequences for failing to act with sufficient expertise, such as **breach of contract**, **accusations of fraud** and **professional negligence**.

- The Fraud Act highlights three offences including abuse of position.

- All information you receive through your work as an accountant should be regarded as **confidential**.

- The **Data Protection Act** gives individuals the right to know what information is held about them. It provides a framework to ensure that personal information is handled properly.

- You are permitted to disclose confidential information in three specific sets of circumstances: when you are properly **authorised** to do so; when you have a **professional** duty to do so; when you have a **legal** duty to do so.

BPP LEARNING MEDIA

Keywords

- **Assurance engagement:** When an accountant provides an opinion that may be relied upon by the client or third parties, for example an external audit report

- **Audit committee:** A sub-committee of a board of directors having non-executive duties overseeing financial reporting duties

- **Breach of contract:** Where a legally binding agreement has been broken by one of the parties

- **Bribery Act 2010:** UK legislation that outlines four offences when bribery occurs

- **Data Protection Act 2018:** Legislation that provides a framework to ensure information is handled properly

- **Disclaimer of liability:** A clause included in an agreement in an attempt to restrict liability or responsibility if someone acts upon or uses an accountant's work

- **Financial interests:** Where an individual or organisation can gain financially from specific activities, for example profit-share schemes

- **Gifts, hospitality and inducements:** Something received that may influence the objectivity of the recipient

- **Information Commissioner's Office (ICO):** A UK authority established to protect public information rights

- **Position of trust:** The professional relationship between accountants and clients where the client has an expectation that the accountant will be acting in the client best interests.

- **Professional distance and independence:** A concept where accountants are and are seen to be separate from their clients

- **Professional negligence:** Failing to act with reasonable skill and care and can result in the payment of compensation to the injured party

- **Sufficient expertise:** Expertise and skill sufficient to complete assignments with in accordance with professional competence and due care

- **UK Fraud Act 2006:** Legislation that specifies three types of fraud offence: false representation, failure to disclose and abuse of position

Test your learning

1   Accepting gifts or hospitality from a client can give rise to which of the following threats to an accountant's fundamental principles?

	✓
Self-interest	
Self-review	
Advocacy	
Familiarity	

2   Being bribed ☐ an offence under the Bribery Act 2010.

3   Notification to the Information Commissioner's Office by data controllers about the processing of personal information is a statutory requirement, and failing to do so is a criminal offence.

	✓
True	
False	

4   Your duty of confidentiality to a client or employer continues even after your contractual relationship with them has ended.

	✓
True	
False	

5   Accountants have a professional duty to disclose confidential information when it is in the public interest and not prohibited by law.

	✓
True	
False	

Taking appropriate action

4

Learning outcomes

1.2	**Explain how to act ethically**
	Students need to know:
	• About specific actions that the accountant may have to take in order to behave ethically
2.7	**Explain the stages in the ethical code's process for ethical conflict resolution**
	Students need to know:
	• How ethical conflict situations could arise in a work context
	• The stages in the process for ethical conflict resolution when a situation presents a conflict in application of the fundamental principles
	• The role of documented organisational policies in preventing ethical conflict from arising
3.2	**Analyse a situation using the conceptual framework and conflict resolution process**
	Students need to be able to:
	• Apply the conceptual framework to a situation
	• Apply the conflict resolution process to a situation
	• Decide when to take advice externally
	• Decide when to refuse to remain associated with the matter creating the conflict, or resign
3.3	**Develop an ethical course of action**
	Students need to be able to:
	• Formulate a specific course of action to address the ethical concerns that have arisen
	• Decide when and how advice about an ethical dilemma or unethical behaviour with regard to their own work, clients, suppliers or colleagues should be sought from a colleague or manager, or from the helpline of the employer or professional body
	• Refer instances of unethical behaviour to responsible persons at work, by reference initially to line management, using discretion and maintaining confidentiality

4.1	**Analyse a situation in light of money laundering law and regulations**
	Students need to know:
	- The possible offences under money laundering law and regulations, and their consequences for accountants and for organisations
	- The events that may occur in relation to the accountant, colleagues, the organisation, its customers and its suppliers that give rise to obligations for the accountant under money laundering law and regulations
	- The consequences for an accountant of failing to act appropriately in response to such events, including the potential for the offences of 'tipping off' and 'failure to disclose'
	- The consequences for any person of 'prejudicing an investigation'
	- The nature of the protection given to accountants by protected disclosures and authorised disclosures under the money laundering law and regulations
	- The position specifically of accountants employed in a business regarding external reporting of the employer's suspected illegal activities under money laundering law and regulations, when the accountant is directly involved, and also when they are not directly involved
4.2	**Identify the relevant body to which questionable behaviour must be reported**
	Students need to know:
	- The nature and role of relevant external authorities in relation to accountants and the money laundering regulations
	- The relevant authority or internal department to which reports about money laundering should be made
	- When and to whom tax errors should be reported
	- The relevant external authorities to which reports about other forms of illegal activity may be made
	- The prescribed internal department and/or external professional body or agency to which reports may be made regarding unethical behaviour and breaches of confidentiality
4.3	**Report suspected money laundering in accordance with the regulations**
	Students need to be able to:
	- Select the information that should be reported by an accountant making a required disclosure in either an internal report or a suspicious activity report (SAR) regarding suspicions about money laundering
	- Identify when the required disclosure should be made

4.4	Decide when and how to report unethical behaviour by employers, colleagues or clients/customers
	Students need to be able to:
	• Identify when it is appropriate to report that a breach of the ethical code has taken place
	• Report in line with formal internal whistle-blowing or 'speak-out' procedures that may be available for reporting unethical behaviour
	• Seek advice confidentially from relevant helplines as appropriate
	• Identify circumstances when there may be public interest disclosure protection available under statute for blowing the whistle externally in the public interest in relation to certain illegal or unethical acts by the employer
	• Seek third-party advice before blowing the whistle externally

Assessment context

You will need to be able to demonstrate your understanding of when to take action on suspicions or knowledge of unethical behaviour. This chapter introduces ethical circumstances that you can meet in the assessment where appropriate action needs to be taken.

Qualification context

As you work through the AAT assessments it is important that you understand what it means to behave ethically. Although you may not be examined explicitly on this elsewhere within the qualification, you will be expected to make the right choices as you work towards becoming a member of the AAT.

Business context

The purpose of this subject is to continue to maintain and enhance the professional reputation and integrity of organisations and the profession as a whole. Knowing when to do the right thing is key to this. There are a number of cases of whistleblowing in the media and you will discover some interesting facts about whistleblowing on the 'public concern at work' website www.pcaw.co.uk.

Chapter overview

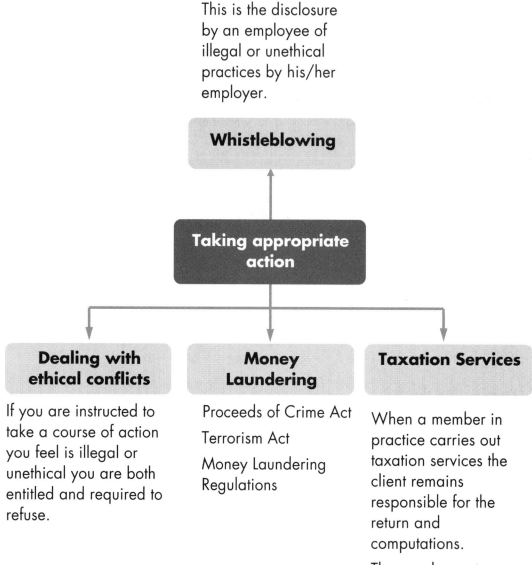

This is the disclosure by an employee of illegal or unethical practices by his/her employer.

Whistleblowing

Taking appropriate action

Dealing with ethical conflicts

If you are instructed to take a course of action you feel is illegal or unethical you are both entitled and required to refuse.

Money Laundering

Proceeds of Crime Act

Terrorism Act

Money Laundering Regulations

Taxation Services

When a member in practice carries out taxation services the client remains responsible for the return and computations.

The member acts as an agent.

Introduction

To be ethical, conduct must also be legal. You need to comply with the law, encourage your colleagues and employers (where relevant) to comply with the law – and advise your clients to comply with the law.

You must remember that the conceptual framework for dealing with ethical dilemmas takes precedence in your professional work. Consider the fundamental ethical principles at risk, identify threats, implement safeguards using professional judgement. If threats cannot be eliminated or reduced to a sufficiently low level the accountant should resign or withdraw from the engagement.

This chapter is all about taking the **appropriate action** and will consider the following areas:

- Identifying appropriate ethical behaviours
- Dealing with ethical conflicts
- Money laundering
- Taxation services
- Whistleblowing

1 Identifying appropriate ethical behaviours

When considering what to do about an ethical issue, first all, consider the application of available legal and ethical guidelines in the particular situation you are facing:

- How might the principles apply?
- Are there any examples or legal precedents that might apply?

If the situation is still unclear, critical decision-making may be required. One method of reaching a conclusion is to:

- **Consider the consequences** – What will be the effects of the course of action – on you and others? A basic test is whether you would feel comfortable if you ever had to defend your course of action at a later date, at court or in the press.

- **Consider your obligations** – What do you 'owe' to other people in the situation or what duty do you have to act in a certain way? A basic test is, would you want to be on the receiving end of any action taken?

The **key questions** are:

(a) Is the action legal and in line with company policy and professional guidelines?

(b) How will it make me feel about myself?

(c) Is the action balanced and fair to all involved?

To help with ethical business cultures, the Institute of Business Ethics (IBE) was established with the aim of encouraging high standards of business behaviour based on the ethical values.

The IBE website www.ibe.org.uk suggests three simple ethical tests for business decisions. We met these tests in an earlier chapter and as a reminder they are:

- **Transparency** ('Do I mind others knowing that I have decided?')
- **Effect** ('Who does my decision affect or hurt?')
- **Fairness** ('Would my decision be considered fair by those affected?')

If, in professional life, you have an ethical concern then normally the most appropriate course of action would be to raise this with your immediate supervisor or employee helpline.

If for any reason this is not possible then seek independent legal advice or contact the relevant professional body for guidance. For AAT members ethical guidance can be sought through the AAT's Ethics Advice line.

Written records should be kept of any discussions and meetings to ensure there is evidence of any advice received. This will help protection in any legal proceedings that may result.

Activity 1: Financial statements and performance

At your firm of chartered accountants, you have been asked by the partner to whom you report to sit in and take notes as she interviews an applicant for the post of receptionist with the firm. In the course of the interview, your attention is drawn to the following aspects of the discussion:

- The partner, having learned that the candidate has three small children, asks lots of questions about her plans to have more children and her childcare arrangements. When the candidate, in return, asks about the firm's family-friendly working policies, you notice that the partner omits to mention the childcare assistance you know is available.

- The candidate reveals that the family depends mainly on income from her husband's job at a local electrical goods manufacturer. As it happens, this company is one of your clients – and you are aware of its plans to shut down the local plant over the coming year.

- The candidate left her previous employers because they continued to employ a successful member of their sales staff who had sexually harassed her and another female employee. This firm is another client of your firm.

After the candidate has left, the partner looks across at you and rolls her eyes and says, 'Just lose those notes, will you?'

Required

What are the ethical issues raised here, and how will you decide what (if anything) to do about them?

2 Dealing with ethical conflicts

At some time in an accountant's career they will have an ethical dilemma to deal with. In situations where the correct course of action is unclear there may be **conflicts of opinion** about what is the 'right thing to do'.

If you are instructed to take a course of action you feel is illegal or unethical you are **both entitled and required to refuse.**

The AAT *Code* (2017) outlines five factors that members should consider when attempting to resolve ethical conflicts. Members should consider the following:

- Relevant facts
- Ethical issues involved
- Fundamental principles related to the matter in question
- Established internal procedures
- Alternative courses of action

In some situations **informal discussion**, perhaps with your supervisor, will resolve the conflict. This method of conflict resolution should be exhausted before taking other steps.

If an informal discussion doesn't resolve the issue, formal internal procedures should be followed.

Member in business	Member in practice
There may be **internal procedures** laid down to deal with situations where conflicts occur.	Where appropriate, seek to resolve the issue through a more formal **discussion** with the **client**.

If the issue is still unresolved:

There may be no option other than **resigning**. The possibility of resignation might in itself persuade the management to change their practice and decisions.	The member should **cease to act** for the client. They should provide a written explanation as to why it was felt necessary.

Internal procedures should always be followed in the first instance. If they do not resolve the issue then a member should consider alternative action. This may include:

- Seeking legal advice
- Contacting the relevant professional body (eg the AAT)

Unless the accountant has a **legal** or **professional duty** to do so, he should not seek to disclose the information and the circumstances surrounding his resignation to third parties.

For an accountant in practice, if a client requests or instructs him to take a course of action that is unethical or illegal you are entitled to refuse. The request may be made in ignorance and good faith and you should attempt to explain the principles that apply. If the client refuses to change then you simply cease to act for that client.

During any resolution process it is important to document the issue together with any discussions held or decisions taken. This is in case your professional body requests evidence on how this conflict was dealt with, or if it is needed in any subsequent legal proceedings.

All accountants have a professional right to disclose any information they consider to be 'in the public interest'. The definition of 'public interest' is extremely vague, so **legal advice** should always be sought to protect the accountant.

In the assessment you may need to identify a potential ethical conflict from information supplied to you. The following activity will get you to think about how you should respond to a conflict once it has been identified.

Activity 2: Sensitive ethical conflict

You are employed as an accounting technician working in practice. You have some concerns regarding inaccuracies in the amounts of time some of your colleagues in practice charge their clients which often results in clients paying for an accountant's time that has not been spent on the client's work. When you report this to the partner she says 'Forget it, the clients are still getting good value for money one way or another. Do you think the partners waste time tying down every hour that goes astray here or there? You worry too much'.

Required:

Consider what ethical conflicts are happening here and what steps you would be required to take.

Illustration 1: Interview process

You have sat in on an interview for the post of receptionist. This candidate, who is very keen and is currently working for another firm of chartered accountants in the city, appears to be the perfect person for the job. As the partner is bringing the interview to a close, the candidate says: 'By the way, I thought you might like to see the kind of systems I've got experience with. Here's a copy, on disk, of our contacts management software.'

After the interview, you tell the partner that you are not comfortable about this. She says that although it is, technically, a breach of copyright, she will destroy the disk after looking over it; this is probably within the definition of 'fair dealing'.

Conclusion:

Potentially the candidate has actually handed her a competing firm's (highly confidential) client/contact list. This would clearly be unethical to accept, let alone use. Does the partner have similar suspicions, or is she acting in ignorance? Did the candidate offer the disk in good faith – or as an incentive to influence the selection decision? You should state your concerns clearly about this. If the partner knowingly takes advantage of unethically-obtained information, and expects you to be silent about it, you are being made party to an unethical course of action; this is a serious ethical conflict, and you should get confidential independent advice on how to deal with it.

Activity 3: Sensitive ethical conflict

Jessica, an AAT member in an accountancy firm, has taken on a new member of staff, Ben. She has noticed that Ben frequently uses the office colour printer to print personal items. This is done during normal office working hours.

Required

Answer the following question by selecting the appropriate option.

In order to behave in a sensitive manner in these circumstances, what is the most appropriate action for Jessica to take immediately?

Action	✓
Report Ben to the AAT.	
Suspend him without pay until further notice.	
Discuss his behaviour with him and encourage him to change it.	

Whenever **conflict of loyalties** arise the legal responsibilities and your professional standards take precedence – although you should use your judgement as to whether they will be seriously compromised enough to take action through any subsequent grievance or ethics procedures.

Sometimes **inappropriate client behaviour** is actually the consequence of an accountant not creating sufficient professional distance between themselves and the client.

Appropriate behaviour is also important outside the workplace and accountants need to ensure they conduct themselves appropriately in their personal lives as well as professionally.

Activity 4: Ethical options to take

Following a presentation to new staff, a trainee approaches you with a query:

'I have a friend who is an AAT member and also the health and safety official at his workplace. He was asked to complete the accident book because someone fell and hurt themselves in the warehouse. He was asked to omit the fact that an ambulance was needed and called. He did what he was told but I think he may have had other options?'

Required

Complete the following sentences by selecting the appropriate options from the choices.

There is a conflict here between the [▼] an accountant owes their employer and their profession. It would be against [▼] not to update

the accident book accurately and to leave out the details of the ambulance could be an unlawful act.

Therefore every effort should be made to persuade the employer to allow full written [⯆] of the accident.

If this is not resolved satisfactorily then [⯆] may be considered and legal advice sought.

Picklist:

consultation
disclosure
duty of care
duty of loyalty
environmental regulations
health and safety regulations
representation
resignation

Activity 5: Ethical options to take

Barry is a professional accountant who works in a mid-sized practice. Two of Barry's clients are both interested in purchasing one particular business and both clients have asked Barry to represent them in their negotiations.

Required

(a) Explain how the fundamental principles can be threatened here.

(b) Describe a possible ethical conflict process that Barry could use to reduce or eliminate any potential threats.

3 Money laundering

A key example of the need to take appropriate action over illegal or unethical activities is the case of **money laundering**.

The key pieces of legislation that form part of the UK anti-money laundering legislation are:

- The Proceeds of Crime Act 2002 (POCA)

- The Terrorism Act 2000 (TA)

- The Money Laundering, Terrorist Financing and Transfer of Funds (Information on the Payer) Regulations 2017 (MLR)

Money laundering is statutorily defined as a crime in the Proceeds of Crime Act (TSO, 2002) when any of the following occurs:

- Concealing, disguising, converting, transferring or removing criminal property

- Taking part in an arrangement to facilitate the acquisition or removing criminal property

- Acquiring, using or possessing criminal property

Assessment focus point

Many times the term **'money laundering'** is associated with a process of transactions in an attempt to make the proceeds appear as if they come from a legitimate source. This can be true in some cases, however the provisions of the Proceeds of Crime Act are much wider and include virtually any involvement in criminal property as a money laundering offence.

Activity 6: Identification of money laundering

You work in a practice as an accounts clerk. Your firm's name is ABC & Co and a part of your role is to maintain the firm's client account recording payments from and to clients. One particular client has been transferring sizable sums of money into the client account at the end of each month for the last six months. Once the money has been transferred into the client account a senior partner returns the money to the client using an ABC & Co cheque. The cheque is signed by the partner and no other signatory is required. You are aware that the client's business is cash based and the client and partner are good friends, knowing each other for many years. You mention to one of your colleagues that it appears strange for these transactions to take place as there seems to be no valid reason for them to occur. Your colleague replies 'Don't concern yourself, we are not doing anything wrong. If this client is in some sort of dodgy business then that's his lookout'

Required

Is there a money laundering issue raised here, and how will you decide what (if anything) to do about these transactions?

Terrorism is defined in the Terrorism Act (TSO, 2000: p. 1) as the use or threat of action designed to influence government, or to intimidate any section of the public, to advance a political, religious or ideological cause where the action would cause violence, threats to health and safety or damage to property including disruption to electronic systems.

There are no **de minimis** (minimum) exceptions to either money laundering or terrorist financing offences. This means that all offences however small must be reported.

The maximum period of imprisonment that can be imposed on a person found guilty of money laundering or terrorist financing is **14 years**. An **unlimited fine** can also be imposed.

Money laundering measures

Financial institutions and non-financial businesses and professions are required to adopt specific measures to help prevent and identify money laundering and terrorist financing, including:

- Implement customer due diligence, keeping information for five years.

- Implement internal reporting measures including an appointment of a **Money Laundering Compliance Principal (MLCP)** and a nominated officer (these can be the same person).

- Avoid doing anything that might prejudice an investigation by 'tipping off' the money launderers.

- Disclose specific knowledge or suspicions to the appropriate authorities.

Proceeds of Crime Act 2002

The Proceeds of Crime Act 2002 (TSO, 2002) created a single set of money laundering offences applicable throughout the UK relating to the proceeds of all crimes, including:

- The principle **money laundering** offences (see above)
- Offences of **failing to report or disclose** suspected money laundering
- Offences of **tipping off** money launderers and prejudicing an investigation

When to disclose?

Under the Proceeds of Crime Act (TSO, 2002) and the Terrorism Act (TSO, 2000), accountants have a duty to report any knowledge or suspicion of money laundering when:

- The accountant knows or has reasonable grounds to suspect that another person is engaged in money laundering.

- The accountant wishes to provide services in relation to property which he or she knows or suspects relates to money laundering or terrorist financing.

Exceptions to duty to report are when the accountant did not obtain the information in the normal course of business (eg a social event outside work) or if the information was obtained in privileged circumstances (eg when providing legal advice).

How to disclose?

If there is an obligation to report (a disclosure), the accountant must disclose as follows:

Type of organisation	Type of report	Given to	Further steps
Partnership, group practice or company	Internal report	Firm's nominated officer	The nominated officer is responsible for deciding whether to make a suspicious activity report (SAR) to the National Crime Agency (NCA).
Sole trader	Suspicious activity report (SAR)	National Crime Agency (NCA)	Not applicable

Information to include in the disclosure

- Identity of suspect (if known)
- Information on which the knowledge or suspicion is based
- Location of laundered property (if known)

Penalty for failure to disclose

A person commits a criminal offence if he/she fails to disclose knowledge or suspicion as soon as practical. The maximum penalty for **failure to disclose** is **five years** in prison or an **unlimited fine**.

For the accountant to be **protected** against accusations of money laundering and for breaches of client confidentiality it is important that the appropriate type of disclosure is made.

Types of disclosures

Type of disclosure	Explanation
Protected disclosure	This is made by someone who knows or suspects another person of money laundering. For example, an accountant who suspects their client of money laundering.
	The accountant will be protected against allegations of breach of confidentiality.
Authorised disclosure	This is made by any person who realises they may have engaged in or be about to engage in money laundering.
	For example, a bank that is asked to transfer money they realise represents the proceeds of crime.

Any person can make an authorised or protected disclosure. However, protected disclosures are compulsory in the regulated sector.

Activity 7: Report to whom? (1)

You work in a large accounting practice and your manager has requested you to set up a direct debit payment for £1,000 per month in respect of 'miscellaneous office expenses'. This type of instruction has not occurred previously and you are surprised to learn that the payment is being made to what appears to be the bank account belonging to your managers' wife.

Required

If you begin to suspect that your manager is using his position in your organisation to launder money, who should you report this to?

	✓
National Crime Agency (NCA)	
The police	
Your firm's nominated officer (providing they are not your manager)	

You are authorised by the AAT to provide bookkeeping services to the public. You operate as a sole trader specialising in giving a quality service to small businesses. One of your clients makes a small living selling bric-a-brac but has just started to also sell second hand high-end laptops. As part of the record keeping you maintain for clients you always take a note of any serial numbers or other unique numbers to identify their inventory. While reading a local newspaper you are concerned to see an article listing a number of serial numbers that relate to stolen laptops. The serial numbers are identical to the laptop details that your bric-a-brac client has been handling.

Required

If you are a sole trader and begin to suspect that one of your clients is laundering money, who should you report this to?

	✓
National Crime Agency (NCA)	
The client	
Nominated officer for money laundering reports	

'Tipping off' offence for accountants

Tipping off is where an accountant informs someone else that an authorised or protected disclosure has been made and this is likely to prejudice any investigation. This is an offence under the Proceeds of Crime Act.

For example, an accountant who tells their client that a notification about that client has been made to National Crime Agency risks committing the offence of tipping off.

The maximum penalty for tipping off is **5 years imprisonment or an unlimited fine**.

'Prejudicing an investigation' offence for all persons

If the investigation is underway or about to start, there is also an offence of **prejudicing an investigation**. This offence can be committed by any person (not just an accountant).

This includes making a disclosure which is likely to hamper an investigation or falsifying, concealing or destroying documents relevant to the investigation.

There is a defence available if the person making this disclosure did not intend to prejudice the investigation.

Activity 9: Money laundering – true or false?

Indicate whether each of the following statements is true or false by selecting the appropriate option.

Description	True ✓	False ✓
If a sole trader suspects money laundering they must disclose this to their nominated officer.		
Conviction of a Money Laundering Regulations offence will give an AAT member a criminal record.		
Telling a client that they have been the subject of a notification to National Crime Agency (NCA) could amount to the criminal offence of tipping off.		

Assessment focus point

In your assessment you may need to identify and explain the appropriate **action** to take in a particular ethical situation. For example, there may be a suspicion that a client has not been under declaring cash sales so potentially involved in money laundering. What should you do? Report to your supervisor? Report internally to your nominated officer? Report externally to the NCA?

The answer will depend on individual circumstances so read tasks carefully! Naturally, the worst course of action would be to do nothing so if you are asked for an action to take then ensure you do suggest one in your answer!

Activity 10: Appropriate action

You have recently visited your client's café business recently and you noticed that they had employed an additional chef – but now, checking the payroll reports, you cannot find any mention of this person, any payments made to her or any other supporting documentation.

Required

What would be the appropriate action to take in these circumstances?

4 Taxation services

Taxation is a complex area. The AAT *Code* does not deal with detailed ethical issues relating to taxation; however, it does provide general principles.

The code (AAT, *2017*) says that:

'A member providing professional tax services has a duty to put forward the best position in favour of a client or an employer.' (p.17)

At the same time, **integrity** and **objectivity** must not be impaired and the service must be **consistent with the law**.

When a member in practice submits a tax return on behalf of a client, it is normally assumed that the member in practice is acting as an agent of the client.

Therefore the responsibilities of the member should be made clear in a letter of engagement.

When carrying out services in relation to taxation it is essential that:

- It is explained that the **client (the principal) remains responsible for the return and computations**; the member is acting as an **agent**

- The responsibilities of the client and member in practice are documented in an engagement letter

- The client receives copies of all computations before submission to the authorities

- The accountant is not involved in the production or submission of false or misleading information

If the member learns there is a material error or omission in a prior year tax return they should:

- Advise the client promptly
- Recommend disclosure to Her Majesty's Revenue & Customs (HMRC)

If the client refuses to do this the member must write to the client informing them they can no longer act for them. The tax authorities should also be informed you are no longer acting for the client.

What happens if funds are retained dishonestly?

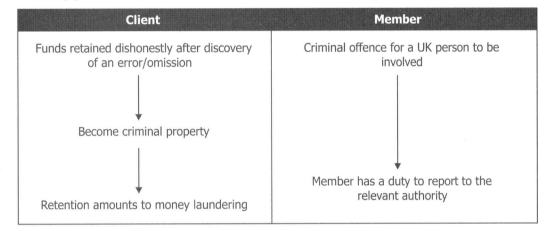

Client	Member
Funds retained dishonestly after discovery of an error/omission	Criminal offence for a UK person to be involved
↓	
Become criminal property	
↓	↓
Retention amounts to money laundering	Member has a duty to report to the relevant authority

Reporting to the relevant authority

After a reasonable time period:

Member in Practice	Member in Business
• Report the situation to the Money Laundering Reporting Officer available. • Or report directly to the National Crime Agency.	If they have acted in relation to the error or omission, they must disclose this to the appropriate authority as soon as possible.
• The member must not disclose this to the client or anyone else, as this may prejudice any investigation.	If they have not acted in relation to the error or omission, they may report it to the appropriate authority. This will not amount to a breach of confidentiality.

The tax authorities in many countries have extensive powers to obtain information.

If the authorities seek to exercise these powers the appropriate course of action for a member is to seek legal advice.

Activity 11: Tax return and appropriate action

James, a member in practice in a large firm of accountants, submits a tax return on behalf of Brian Ltd.

Required

(a) **Complete the following sentence by selecting the appropriate option.**

In this situation, James is acting as [_____ ▼] of Brian Ltd.
Brian Ltd is [_____ ▼].

Picklist:
an agent
HM Revenue & Customs
the principal

(b) **Complete the following sentence by selecting the appropriate option.**

Six months later, James becomes aware that there is a known error in Brian Ltd's tax return. He advises his client to disclose this to HMRC. However, having given the directors at Brian Ltd reasonable time to do this, they still refuse to make the disclosure.

James is obliged to report the client's refusal and the facts surrounding it to [_____ ▼].

Picklist:

HM Revenue & Customs
the Money Laundering Reporting Officer
the National Crime Agency

Activity 12: Tax savings

What should you do if a client asks you how much tax you will be able to save them this year?

	✓
Provide them with an estimate based on what you achieved last year.	
Tell them that you will save them as much as possible.	
Tell them that you cannot provide such information.	

Activity 13: Significant tax errors

What should you do if become aware of a significant error in a tax return that you prepared and submitted for a client in a previous year?

	✓
Do nothing as admitting errors will damage your professional reputation.	
Correct the error by adjusting this year's tax return to compensate.	
Tell the client to advise HMRC about the error.	

5 Whistleblowing

This is the disclosure by an employee of illegal or unethical practices by his or her employer.

Employers will have confidentiality and disclosure policies in place, however protection is offered to employees, ensuring they cannot be dismissed for disclosing confidential information internally or to the appropriate regulator.

The **Public Information Disclosure Act (TSO, 1998: p.1)(PIDA)** states that whistleblowers will be protected provided the disclosure is in good faith and they have reasonable grounds to believe:

- The law is being breached
- The health or safety of any individual is endangered
- The environment is being damaged
- Information on any of the above is being concealed

Assessment focus point

Accountants have a responsibility to act in the **public interest** and a part of this obligation includes reporting or disclosing unethical behaviour whenever identified, for example pollution in excess of regulations. Two real life examples is where a whistleblower has made allegations that the oil company Royal Dutch Shell had not disclosed all information on two large oil spills in Nigeria. Staying with the theme of oil, an engineer 'whistleblowed' and made public that a cruise ship belonging to Prince Cruise Lines had illegally disposed oil waste off the English coast. Misappropriation of public money can also be an area where an individual may consider there is need to 'go public'. Confidentiality is not breached when disclosure is in the public interest so look out for these types of situations on the assessment.

Before whistleblowing externally, the issue of concern should be discussed internally with management.

Many large organisations will have an ethics committee. This is a committee that will help set ethical standards and provide guidance on ethical issues. If an ethics committee is available, they should be consulted. This may resolve the issue.

Whistleblowing should be a last resort option. Before getting to the whistleblowing stage it advisable to take third party advice. For example, contacting the AAT's Ethics Advice line and taking legal advice. Remember, the principles of confidentiality and loyalty are important to the profession.

Where a whistleblower is victimised or dismissed, he or she can bring a claim for damages to an employment tribunal.

Confidentiality or 'gagging' clauses in employment contracts (that stop an employee from speaking out) are void if the employee is protected by the Act.

Activity 14: Whistleblowing and appropriate actions

Anna is being put in a difficult situation. Her manager is deliberately concealing evidence of corruption and criminal activity.

Required

(a) Answer the following questions by selecting the appropriate option.

Description	True ✓	False ✓
The manager's behaviour is in the interests of the public.		
Anna's ability to work with the appropriate level of professional competence and due care is being compromised.		
Providing she acts in good faith she will be protected under the Public Interest Disclosure Act.		

(b) Answer the following question by selecting the appropriate options from the picklist below.

What action should Anna take in this situation? Place the steps in sequential order.

Action	Steps in sequential order
Initial action	
If further action is needed	

Picklist:

Report internally (where procedures exist)
Report externally
Report in due course

- Generally speaking, ethical conduct is **legal conduct**.

- When making an ethical decision, it can help to (i) consider the **consequences** and (ii) consider your own **obligations**.

- A **basic test** is to consider whether you want to be on the receiving end of whatever action you are about to take.

- If you are employed by an organisation, any matter of ethical concern should be raised with your **immediate supervisor**. If you are self-employed, you may need to seek **independent advice**.

- As an accountant you are required to be vigilant for instances of **money laundering** – the attempt to conceal the identity of money created as a consequence of illegal activities.

- Particular ethical issues are raised by performing **taxation services**. When you submit a tax return or computations for a client or employer, you are acting as an agent of the taxpayer.

- You have a **duty** to put forward the best position, in favour of your employer or client. You also have a duty towards the tax authorities to provide information in good faith.

- In any **conflict of loyalties**, the requirements of the law and your professional standards take precedence – although you should use your judgement as to whether they will be seriously compromised enough to take action through grievance or ethics procedures.

- If you are asked, instructed or encouraged to take a course of action that is illegal, or unethical by the standards of your profession, you are **entitled and required to refuse**.

- If you suspect that your employers have committed or may commit an illegal or significant unethical act, your first aim is to persuade them to stop or to put the matter right. If they do not, you may have to make a **disclosure** to an appropriate regulator – but you should seek **independent legal advice**.

- Many instances of **inappropriate client behaviour** are actually consequences of an accountant not creating sufficient professional distance between themselves and the client. It is also important for an accountant to conduct themselves appropriately in their personal lives.

- **Whistleblowing** is the disclosure by an employee of illegal or unethical practices by his or her employer.

Keywords

- **Agent:** Often used in a taxation context where the accountant acts as an agent or representative of a client

- **Authorised disclosure:** A disclosure made by the money launderer him or herself when they realise they have been or are going to be involved in money laundering.

- **De minimis:** A Latin expression that means there is no minimum limit therefore for money laundering and terrorism financing of any value will be a criminal offence

- **Ethical conflict:** Where there is an ethical disagreement, conflict or dilemma and where a course of action will need to be decided upon

- **Failure to disclose:** A criminal offence that occurs when an individual does not report specific information or suspicions of money laundering or terrorist financing

- **Money laundering:** A criminal offence that can cover a broad range of activities or arrangements when dealing in criminal property

- **Money Laundering Regulations *2017* (MLR):** Outlines the measures in preventing the use of the financial system for money laundering purposes

- **Money Laundering Compliance Principal (MLCP):** A designated officer, who is a member of the Board of Directors, within an organisation who has expert knowledge of money laundering

- **Nominated officer:** The individual nominated to receive internal suspicious activity reports and who assesses whether a suspicious activity report should be made to the National Crime Agency (NCA)

- **Principal:** Often used in a taxation context and is the client in an 'accountant and client' relationship

- **Proceeds of Crime Act 2002 (POCA):** UK legislation that outlines money laundering offences and maximum penalties

- **Protected disclosure:** A disclosure made by someone who has knowledge or suspicions of another individual who has or is going to be engaged in money laundering

- **Public Information Disclosure Act 1998 (PIDA):** Provides protection for those who breach confidentiality on the grounds of public interest

- **Suspicious activity report (SAR):** An external report made to the appropriate authorities, for example the National Crime Agency, disclosing information or suspicions on suspected money laundering

- **Terrorism Act 2000 (TA):** UK legislation that outlines offences connected with terrorist financing and money laundering

- **Tipping off:** A situation where an investigation is prejudiced as someone has informed a suspected money launderer that an investigation is being or may be undertaken

- **Whistleblowing:** A disclosure made in the public interest regarding unethical or illegal practices

Test your learning

1 A self-employed accountant with an ethical dilemma should seek advice from:

	✓
One of the accountant's employees with ethics training	
The ethics advice line of their professional body or a close friend	
An independent legal expert or the ethics advice line of their professional body	

2 The maximum period of imprisonment for committing the offence of tipping off is:

	✓
5 years	
7 years	
14 years	

3 Which party is responsible for the accuracy of facts, information and computations used by an accountant performing tax work for a client?

	✓
The client	
The accountant	

4 If you are an employed member of a professional body you owe a duty of loyalty to:

	✓
Your profession and HMRC	
Your employer and your client	
Your employer, your profession and the public interest	

5 In a working in practice situation, if a client requests or instructs you to take a course of action that is unethical or illegal, you are entitled and required in the first instance to:

	✓
Terminate the appointment at once	
Refuse	
Report your client to the relevant authorities	

Activity answers

CHAPTER 1 The principles of ethical working

Activity 1: Benefits and drawbacks of following the *AAT Code of Professional Ethics*

Description	Benefit ✓	Drawback ✓
Cost of increased work		✓
Restriction on services you can provide		✓
Job satisfaction	✓	
Better reputation	✓	
Increased workload		✓
Protection from negligence claims	✓	

Activity 2: Ethical tests of effect

When considering effect, the employee will ask himself or herself:

Who does my decision affect or hurt?

Activity 3: Unethical but not illegal

Possible answers can include but not limited to:

- Use of zero hour employment contracts.
- 'Sweatshop' style manufacturing processes
- Using a non-renewable resource (eg coal) when a renewable resource is available (eg solar power).
- Pressurised selling techniques (eg repeated unsolicited telephone calls).
- Allowing customers to purchase an inappropriate product for their requirements (eg an incorrect mobile telephone tariff).
- Leaving machinery running when not required (eg not turning off bus engines when idling).
- Employees travelling separately to a meeting when they could share a car.
- Conserving energy (eg leaving windows open and letting heat escape).

Activity 4: Code of Ethics – true or false?

Statement	True ✓	False ✓
The *AAT Code of Professional Ethics* is legally enforceable.		✓
The *AAT Code of Professional Ethics* is an example of criminal law.		✓
Breach of the *AAT Code of Professional Ethics* on the marketing of professional services will give an AAT member a criminal record.		✓

The *AAT Code of Professional Ethics* is **not** legally enforceable in its own right. However, failure to follow it could have professional consequences and be used as evidence of other wrongdoing (eg fraud).

Activity 5: Internal code of conduct

Possible answers can include but not limited to:

- Fundamental principles to be adhered to, for example integrity and honesty in business dealings

- How to deal with conflicts of interest, for example when representing two clients who have shared financial interests

- How disciplinary actions are dealt with and rights to appeal

- Dress code expected of employees

- Policy on accepting gifts from customers or clients

- Protection of confidential information

- Health and safety procedures

- Private use of employer resources, for example printing

- Equal opportunities, for example vacancy advertising policy

- How to report unethical issues within the practice

Activity 6: Sponsoring bodies

(a)

Organisation	✓
ICAS	✓
ACCA	
FRC	
CIPFA	✓

(b)

Statement	✓
The FRC regulates the global accountancy profession.	
The FRC issues standards for professionals involved in audit and assurance work.	✓
The FRC has the authority to discipline accountants who do not observe actuarial standards.	✓

Activity 7: Fundamental ethical principles and scenarios

Scenario	Fundamental principle and explanation
Tom is a journalist who writes articles for a financial newspaper and has been recommending his readers to purchase shares in companies that he holds shares in.	Objectivity is relevant here. This is because Tom's readers might be encouraged to purchases shares in the companies that Tom has a financial interest in. If enough readers purchase the recommended shares this can increase the share prices for the benefit of Tom.
A member of a professional body has been caught speeding while driving to a client meeting. The speeding offence has been reporting in the local media naming both the member's name and professional body membership.	Members of professional bodies are expected to behave in a professional manner in their professional and private life. The behaviour of the member here would bring disrepute not only upon themselves but to their professional body as well.
Toni is a junior member of staff and has been requested to complete a complex sales ledger reconciliation. Normally, the work should take two days, however Toni has been allocated one morning to complete the work.	Professional competence and due care is relevant here. Although, Toni may be doing her best to provide a good service in completing the reconciliation she may have neither the expertise or experience to complete this work. As there is not enough time available to complete the work in the normal time of two days Toni will be rushing to complete and may make errors in its completion.

Scenario	Fundamental principle and explanation
A partner in a firm of accountants has spent 40 hours working on a client's financial statements. Before an invoice is sent to the client the partner notices that 80 hours have been used for the invoice calculation. The partner allows the invoice to be sent based on 80 hours instead of 40 hours.	Integrity is relevant here. This is because the partner is not being honest in allowing an inflated invoice to be sent to the client.
Jackie is an accountant specialising in tax dispute cases. As a marketing initiative Jackie has posted details of successful cases on her accountancy practice website. To help with authenticity Jackie has used the real names of past and present clients without their permission.	Confidentiality is relevant here as confidential client information should not be released in this way without client consent. The confidentiality principle also applies to past and present clients information.

Activity 8: Threats to the fundamental principles

Scenario	Ethical threat and explanation
Steve is a member in practice. He is currently engaged on an assurance assignment with Potter plc. On Sunday he celebrated his successful completion of his AAT training. As a gift his grandmother has transferred her 2% shareholding in Potter plc to him.	This is an example of a self-interest threat as Steve will now have a personal interest in the financial results of Potter plc. There is no evidence that Steve will falsify figures in any way however it is important for members to be seen as independent as possible.
The accountant at JED has been taken ill. JED's audit firm has been asked to prepare the financial statements and audit the financial statements.	This is an example of self-review as the audit firm will be checking its own work. A safeguard here is to have two different teams working on the assignment.
Charles Greenfield has been the engagement partner on the audit of Hamptons for many years.	This is a familiarity threat as the partner conducting the audit may have established too close a relationship with the company. A possible safeguard here would be to rotate partners on the audit.

Activity 9: Identifying threats to the ethical principles

Garden centres

There is an objectivity issue here. There is a financial incentive here for you to value the company incorrectly. If you valued the company on the low side then one of your business partners would have an opportunity to acquire the company for less than it is actually worth.

There are also issues of professional competence and due care. Even if you had no intention of buying the company, because you specialise in tax work, you may not have the right skills to carry out the valuation accurately.

If you were to carry out the valuation for the garden centre, given your interest in acquiring this type of business your objectivity could be called into question. You have an obligation to treat people fairly and with honesty and therefore you should decline the engagement.

If you had no business interest in the valuation of the garden centre you still owe the brothers a duty of care. As you have little experience valuing businesses you should recommend somebody else from your firm to undertake this task.

Hair salon

There is an integrity issue here. You have been undercharged for work carried out on your behalf. The fact that it is due to a mistake by the hair salon owner does not make it right.

The consequences of not telling the hair salon owner would be that your firm would be £600 better off. However, you have an obligation to pay the agreed fair share you verbally contracted to. It would be dishonest to keep quiet on this matter. You should at the earliest opportunity contact the hair salon and tell them they have made a mistake.

Software developer

There is an objectivity issue here. If you were to recommend the investment opportunity in the property company solely due to your relationship with the principal you would not be acting independently. Your friendship may lead you to be biased in your advice to the software developer.

The software developer is expecting independent advice. If you were to tell him about the opportunity of investing in the property company you should fully disclose your relationship with the owner. You have an obligation to be impartial and to make it clear that you have limited expertise in this area.

Your team mate

There are issues of professional competence and due care here. Any answer you were to give on the spot would risk being incomplete, inaccurate or out of date. This could have serious consequences if your team mate acts on your advice.

Any advice you give on the spur of the moment may be acted upon. You should set up a time when you can give this matter your full attention before you make any suggestions or give any advice. Suggest your team mate comes into your office for a meeting.

Your father in law

There is a confidentiality issue here as you need the client's authority to disclose financial information before it has become a matter of public record even to members of your family.

You have a duty of care to your client. You should not disclose any information relating to your client until it has become a matter of public record.

Your plumber

If the plumber is VAT registered and you are have grounds to suspect that payment of VAT is being avoided then there are issues of integrity and professional behaviour. You are held to a set of ethical guidelines by your professional body and you are accountable even outside your workplace. If you agree to the plumber's suggestion you may be helping him commit tax evasion.

If you believe the plumber is giving you the discount for cash so he can avoid paying VAT you should pay with a cheque or hire another, more reputable plumber. You must not become a party to tax evasion as it is against the law.

Activity 10: Identifying the Nolan principles

Description	Principle
Holders of public office should be as open as possible about all the decisions and actions that they take. They should give reasons for their decisions.	Openness
Holders of public office should not place themselves under any financial or other obligation to outside individuals or organisations that might seek to influence them in the performance of their official duties.	Integrity
Holders of public office have a duty to declare any private interests relating to their public duties and take steps to resolve any conflicts arising in a way that protects the public interest.	Honesty
Holders of public office should promote and support these principles by leadership and example.	Leadership
Holders of public office are accountable for their decisions and actions. They must submit themselves to whatever scrutiny is appropriate to their office.	Accountability
Holders of public office should act solely in terms of the public interest. They should not do so in order to gain financial or other material benefit for themselves, their family or their friends.	Selflessness
In carrying out public business (eg making public appointments, recommending individuals for rewards and benefits), holders of public office should make choices on merit.	Objectivity

Activity 11: Types of operational risk

Example	Type of operational risk
Misappropriation of assets	Internal fraud
Theft of information	External fraud
Discrimination	Employment practices
Knowingly selling products with defects	Business practices
Vandalism	Damage to physical assets
Using pirated software that contains bugs	Business disruption
Inaccurate or misleading reporting	Process and delivery outputs
Loss of confidence by the public	Reputational risk
Damages paid to customers for injury caused by a faulty product	Legal or litigation risk

Activity 12: Misconduct investigation

Circumstance	Conclusive proof of misconduct ✓	Not conclusive proof of misconduct ✓
Harrison unreasonably refused to co-operate with an investigation into his conduct.	✓	
Harrison failed to reply to correspondence from the AAT on one occasion.		✓

Activity 13: The AAT CPD Cycle

The AAT's CPD cycle comprises four steps: assess, | **plan** |, action and evaluate.

Activity 14: CPD in practice

(a) Professional competence and due care is associated with keeping skills up to date and maintaining skills and knowledge will help safeguard confidentiality, professional behaviour and objectivity.

(b) There are many potential answers here and possible suggestions can include (but not limited to) money laundering rules, regulation of the accountancy profession, tax legislation and accounting and reporting standards for small and medium sized companies.

Activity 15: Triple bottom line model

	Possible suggestions
Economic (financial)	Taking into account costs and benefits in implementing sustainability policies. For example, the cost of installing solar panels and the associated savings in electricity costs.
	Maintaining profitability by changing with market developments and investing in research and development.
	Suppliers, for example by paying suppliers promptly will help suppliers to be sustainable financially.
Social	The wellbeing of staff, for example employing locally and training staff. Suppliers, for example using local suppliers who use sustainable processes.
	Also by taking into account the views of the local community when making decisions, for example taking into account the views of local residents before building a multi-floor office
Environmental	Looking at opportunities to reduce pollution. For example, using virtual meeting technology instead of travelling to and from client premises

Activity 16: Suggestions for sustainability

There are many valid answers here and possible suggestions can include:

- Power down computers at the end of the working day or when not being used

- Encourage cycling to work or car sharing schemes

- Ensure the office is adequately insulated

- Discourage unnecessary printing of emails

- Recycle paper wherever possible

- Use energy-saving light bulbs and automatically activated lighting systems

- Use local suppliers and pay fair prices
- Employ locally and support apprenticeship scheme participation
- Having a sustainable business model by keeping up with market trends and new technology

CHAPTER 2 Behaving in an ethical manner – part I

Activity 1: Unethical and dishonest behaviour

Examples of some dishonest behaviour can include:

- Stealing property
- Using company information for personal gain
- Knowingly selling products with defects
- Damage to physical assets – vandalism
- Using pirated software
- Deliberately producing inaccurate or misleading information

Activity 2: Behaviour and appropriate action

(a)

	✓
Report him to the AAT.	
Dismiss him.	
Discuss this with him in private and ask him to refrain from logging on to Facebook during working hours.	✓

(b)

	✓
Integrity	
Discretion	✓
Honesty	

Activity 3: Five threats to the fundamental principles

Threat
Intimidation: There is a clear threat of intimidation as Jake has threatened Ella with losing her job if she cannot fulfil the purchases needed for next season demand.
Familiarity: There is a threat of familiarity as Ella is purchasing the garments from a family member meaning there is a personal relationship that may influence Ella's decision.

Threat
Self-interest: There is a financial incentive of £0.50 per garment if Ella chooses her Uncle as a supplier. As 1,000 garments have been ordered this amounts to £500 for Ella.
Self-review: Ella has self-checked the invoice and passed on for payment. If Jake had Jake had checked the invoice it is likely that the higher price charged for last season's styles would have been identified.
Advocacy: Ella is putting forward to Jake a justification and point of view for her actions that are unduly influenced by the other threats identified.

Activity 4: Potential threat to fundamental ethical principles

	✓
Self-review	
Intimidation	✓
Familiarity	
Advocacy	

Activity 5: Safeguards to reduce threats

THREATS	POSSIBLE SAFEGUARDS
Self-interest	
Financial interest in a client (eg owning shares).	• Sell the shares. • Remove the individual concerned from the assurance engagement. • Resign from the engagement.
Undue dependence on the client for fee income.	A firm should have policies to monitor and manage the reliance on revenue received from a single client.
Close business relationship with a client.	A firm should advise staff that they must be independent from assurance clients.

Self-review	
Preparing a subject matter (eg financial statements) and then performing assurance work on them (eg an audit)	Use different partners and engagement teams with separate reporting lines for the provision of non-assurance service to an assurance client.

Self-review	
A member of the assurance team has recently been employed by the client, and was in a position to exert significant influence over the subject matter.	This individual should not work on the assurance engagement for this client, until an appropriate time period has elapsed.

Advocacy	
Acting as an advocate on behalf of an assurance client in litigation, or disputes with third parties	Do not perform assurance work.

Familiarity	
A member of the engagement team having a close relationship with the client	A firm should advise staff that they must be independent from assurance clients.
Accepting gifts from a client	Only accept the gift if clearly insignificant.
Long association of senior personnel with the assurance client	Rotate senior assurance team personnel.

Intimidation	
Being threatened with dismissal on a client engagement	• Involve an additional member to review the work performed.
An assurance client indicating they will not award a planned non-assurance contract if the member in practice disagrees with the client on an issue	• Publish clear procedures to encourage staff to communicate such issues at senior levels within the firm.
Being threatened with litigation	• Consult an independent third party, such as a committee or independent directors, or professional regulatory body or another member.

Activity 6: Fundamental ethical principles threatened in business

Integrity – providing false figures on a VAT return is dishonest, misleading and fraudulent

Objectivity – bribes and intimidation can adversely affect objectivity and professional judgement

Professional behaviour – the behaviour of the director and the submission of falsified VAT figures would bring the individuals involved, the company and the accountancy profession into disrepute

Activity 7: Safeguards in business

A business's authorisation policy states that purchase requisitions over £100 must be signed by two different employees.

This part of the policy is primarily designed to

reduce the risk of employees misappropriating business assets .

Activity 8: New client relationship

	✓
How profitable the relationship will be	
Whether acceptance would create any threats to compliance with the fundamental principles	✓
Whether the client's directors meet the firm's moral and ethical standards	

Activity 9: Customer due diligence – true or false

(a)

Statement	Explanation
Hubert can verify the client's identity through an informal discussion with the chief accountant.	This statement is false as the client's identity must be verified by valid documentation. The chief accountant's evidence cannot be relied upon as not independent and is not be substantiated as correct.
If due diligence is not possible Hubert can still perform professional services for this client for two years.	This statement is false because if due diligence is not possible before taking on a new client before services can be supplied.

(b)

Statement	✓
Notify the police of the relationship	
Verify the client's identity on the basis of documents, data or other reliable information	✓
Verify the nature and value of the client's assets	

Activity 10: Customer due diligence and existing clients

Customer due diligence should be carried out as these requests are inconsistent with the previous knowledge of the client's business affairs. There is a change in the industry sector with a potentially large investment involved. Accountants have an ethical duty to undertake customer due diligence for both new and existing clients when there is a possible risk to the fundamental ethical principles.

Activity 11: Conflict of interest and two clients

There is a conflict of interest as a situation may arise where the accountant has to act for one of the clients to the detriment of the other. This may be due to a breach of confidentiality or perhaps a self-interest threat. Safeguards that be put in place can include; using two separate engagement teams, supervision and review by senior personnel, and taking advice from independent third parties. If the conflict of interest risk is significant cannot be reduced to an acceptable level then it may be advisable to withdraw from of the engagements to eliminate the risk.

Activity 12: Low fees

Ethical threat	Fundamental principle
Self-interest	Professional competence and due care

Activity 13: Conflict of interest and fees

(a)

Questions	Solutions
Could it be misleading to refer to your accountancy practice as the 'best in the region'?	Yes
Why is this the case?	'Best' is ambiguous and difficult to prove

(b)

Description	True ✓	False ✓
If the fees are set too low, this may result in a reduction in the quality of the work undertaken.	✓	
It is unethical to offer a free initial consultation.		✓
Other accountancy services should not be offered for free as the quality of work may be compromised if accountants receive no fee or a reduced fee.	✓	

BPP
LEARNING MEDIA

Activity 1: Financial statements and performance

Question	Solution
How do we know how a company has performed over the year?	Financial statements
Who is responsible for preparing the financial statements?	Company (management)
Do they have an incentive to manipulate the figures?	Yes (bonuses)
How do we measure whether the financial statements are reasonable?	(International) Financial Reporting Standards
Who are the primary users of the financial statements?	Shareholders (owners of the company)
How do they know they can rely on the financial statements?	Auditors (eg they will test the numbers and associated narrative)

Activity 2: Gifts, hospitality and inducements

	✓
Yes – members in practice are entitled to receive any gift offered by a client, regardless of the value of the gift.	
Yes – the offer is made to Harry and all other suppliers, and the gift is not significant enough to influence his judgement.	✓
No – the gift is significant, and could be perceived as likely to influence his judgement.	

Activity 3: Independence in practice

(a)

	✓
Independence in mind	
Independence in appearance	
Independence in both mind and appearance	✓

(b)

Description	True ✓	False ✓
Members in practice must demonstrate they are independent of assurance clients by applying a rigid set of rules.		✓
Members in practice must demonstrate they are independent of assurance clients by taking a conceptual framework approach to independence.	✓	

Activity 4: Factors to consider when accepting hospitality

Whether this is an ethical issue depends on a number of factors, such as:

- **The value of the hospitality:** A sporting event would not normally be regarded as significant – but it would depend on how lavish the package was (or rare the tickets).

- **The circumstances:** In this case, the fact that the host is bidding for a major contract might suggest an attempt to influence the decision.

- In this case, there is probably no ethical issues as you might not be the one with authority to make the decision.

- However, due to the fact the tickets are likely to be in high demand and have a high value, and the circumstances, it is likely to be an issue for higher management.

Activity 5: Identifying bribes

Scenario	Explanation
You meet an old friend in a bar who works for another audit firm. During your chat she offers to buy you another drink if you would explain how a spreadsheet formula could be used in her audit work.	This would probably not be seen as a bribe. The drink is a very low value item and the information supplied is general and not specific to a specific set of circumstances and the advantage of using the formula would likely to be minimal.
You are an accounting technician working in practice and a senior partner from another accountancy firm telephones you and offers you a seat in a box at a Premier League football match. You wasn't sure at the time as the line was bad but the partner also mentioned something about a client list.	This would be seen as a bribe as the football match seat would have a high monetary value. The partner is implying that if the seat is supplied then a client list would need to be provided. This could be of particular interest to a rival firm who may not be acting to the best of ethics. If the client list was supplied this would also breach confidentiality.

Scenario	Explanation
Your team has been working long hours to ensure a deadline is met for the submission of a client's financial statements. The financial statements were submitted with a day to spare. The client admits that it was his bad record keeping that caused this delayed submission and as a thank you insists on taking the whole team out for a chicken meal. As your team has twenty members this could be expensive for the client.	In probability this would not be seen to be a bribe. The work has already been completed and the offer is open to all members of the team and just to one or two individuals. Although, the final bill for the meal may be expensive per team member the cost would not be excessive.
One of your clients is in the process of applying for a large bank loan. Although, you have only known the client for a month the client has asked you to supply a reference to the bank stating that you have known her for three years. The client has mentioned she has a luxury apartment in Spain that she normally lets out to holidaymakers but you are welcome to use this free of charge during August.	This would like a bribe to a third party as the luxury apartment would have a high rental value especially during the summer months. The inaccurate bank reference could be seen to be fraudulent as the bank is relying on a three year reference to extend a large loan to the client.

Activity 6: Safeguards to reduce threats

Threats	Possible safeguard
Insufficient time to spend on duties	Ensuring there is adequate time to spend on duties
	Not taking on the role unless you know you have the time to perform the duties properly
Inadequate information to perform the duties properly	Obtaining the necessary information (through consultation with superiors in the organisation)
Insufficient experience or knowledge	Additional advice from someone with the expertise, or training
Inadequate resources	Obtaining the necessary resources (through consultation with superiors in the organisation)

Activity 7: Inadequate information and consequences

	Explanation
Which of the fundamental principles are most threatened here?	Due care is most at risk here as Marcy has been reckless in preparing the financial statements without having sufficient information. Integrity is also threatened as Marcy should have been honest to Dan about these circumstances. Acting in this manner can also breach professional behaviour as this can bring disrepute to Marcy, and the accountancy profession including Marcy's professional body.
If Dan receives a fine due to these financial statements, on what grounds could Dan receive compensation from Marcy?	Breach of contract through professional negligence.

Activity 8: Types of fraud

Type of offence	✓
Fraud by false representation	
Fraud by failing to disclose information	
Fraud by abuse of position	✓

This is the most likely offence as Julie has abused her position when holding the money on behalf of Pickering, as it appears Julia has been using the money for her own interests.

Activity 9: Duty of confidentiality and disclosure

Questions	Yes or No
Disclosure if Derek has broken criminal laws	Yes (must disclose)
Disclosure that is not required by law but which is authorised by Derek	Yes (can disclose)

Activity 10: Duty of confidentiality and disclosure

Questions	Solution
In what circumstances is Thomas under an obligation to disclose information about his client?	Disclosure is required by law
If disclosure is required by law and Thomas refuses to co-operate, is he committing a criminal offence?	Yes

Activity 11: Duty of confidentiality and disclosure

Question	Solution
Should Martin register with the Information Commissioner?	Yes
The reason for this is that Martin	Holds personal information

Activity 12: Disclose or not to disclose

(1) Jane as a legal obligation to disclose and cooperate fully with the HMRC on this matter. If Jane did not answer HMRC's questions fully and disclose all relevant information here Jane would be implicating herself in this fraudulent activity. There is a criminal element also in this instance as this will also money laundering and the money incorrectly reclaimed from the HMRC would effectively be criminal property. Jane should also has a professional duty to disclose all information here as any member involved in this type of activity would bring disrepute not only on themselves but also to the membership body and the wider accountancy profession.

(2) Jane would have a public interest duty to disclose the blocked fire exit to the trading officer. Health and safety is of paramount importance and especially so in situations where the general public would be unware that such a risk exists. If a fire was to start and resulted in injury or worse there could also be criminal and civil actions taken against anyone who did not take any action to help prevent this outcome.

(3) Jane should refuse to disclose this information as this is sensitive information and confidential to the business. Jane may wish to refer this matter to the hotel's owner for him or her to make a decision on whether to allow this information to be disclosed in this way.

CHAPTER 4 Taking appropriate action

Activity 1: Financial statements and performance

The partner's focus on family responsibilities may be construed as sexual discrimination under UK law – unless she asks the same questions of any men she interviews for the job.

Giving incomplete information about the organisation might be more significantly unethical if its effect was to mislead someone into taking employment under false pretences. In this case, not much harm is being done, as the candidate is merely being influenced against accepting a job that she probably will not be offered.

You may feel sorry for the family, who are unaware that the husband will soon lose his job. But this is a fact of economic life – and you have the overriding duty of confidentiality not to disclose what you know about the client's plans.

The behaviour of the candidate's previous employer is unethical. But you have come by the information indirectly – and is it anything to do with you? It would certainly be in your client's best interests not to risk legal claims against them.

The partner's request to you to 'lose' the notes is ambiguous. It sounds unethical – whether as a suggestion of prejudice against the candidate, or as a way of dodging responsibility for the ethical issues raised.

So what might you do? First you might decide to clarify exactly what the partner meant; this would clear up any misunderstanding, and highlight the ethical issues more clearly. It might also be possible to draw her attention (respectfully) to the risks of her interview questions being construed as discrimination.

Other than this, it may not be your place to do much more – although you may choose to advise your clients of the ethical and legal considerations that have come to your attention: the need to be socially responsible in notifying employees as early as possible of impending redundancies and the need for consistency, fairness and compliance with regard to disciplinary issues (such as sexual harassment).

Activity 2: Sensitive ethical conflict

Your answer should acknowledge that there is an ethical conflict here if this matter is pursued. If this behaviour is ignored then this would compromise your professional ethics of integrity and honesty. It is worrying that the partner is insisting that you let the matter drop and indicates the culture of the firm, from the top down, is clearly unsympathetic to what are seen as 'minor' ethical concerns. If the firm has one you may need to go to the ethics committee, which should have impartial members, or obtain independent third party advice on how to take the matter further.

Activity 3: Sensitive ethical conflict

Action	✓
Report Ben to the AAT.	
Suspend him without pay until further notice.	
Discuss his behaviour with him and encourage him to change it.	✓

Activity 4: Ethical options to take

There is a conflict here between the | **duty of loyalty** | an accountant owes to their employer, and their profession. It would be against | **health and safety regulations** | not to update the accident book accurately and to leave out details of the ambulance could be an unlawful act. Therefore every effort should be made to persuade the employer to allow full written | **disclosure** | of the accident. If this is not resolved satisfactorily then | **resignation** | many be considered and legal advice sought.

Activity 5: Ethical options to take

(a) The two principles most at risk here are **objectivity** and **confidentiality**. Working for two clients it may be difficult for Barry to complete his work without being biased towards one client or the other. He will also need to be careful of confidentiality as he will have information that could be valuable to either client.

These are not only the risks here as integrity or honesty can also be threatened as Barry would need to be open and transparent to both clients – but without breaching confidentiality!

(b) (1) Establish all threats and risks to principles.

(2) Review the firm's procedures and code of ethics for guidance.

(3) Seek advice from a senior partner or professional body.

(4) Identify any safeguards to be put in place, for example a colleague may be able to act on behalf of one of the clients instead, use of Chinese walls, senior partner reviews, confidentiality agreements or even decline one of the engagements.

Activity 6: Identification of money laundering

There certainly appears to be a suspicion of money laundering here as it looks as though the client is using the firm's client account to convert cash into a cheque to pay subsequently into a bank account. As the cheques will be coming from a respected source, ie ABC & Co's cheques, this will give the impression of respectability. The question is why the client doesn't simply pay their cash into their own bank account rather than using this circular transaction. There can be a threat of familiarity here as the partner and client have a connection beyond the normal accountant/client relationship. The colleague is incorrect in the statement as the partner and ABC & Co (plus possibly ABC Co's employees too) will be implicated in money laundering as the client account is being used to convert possibly criminal money. We look at disclosure later in chapter 4, however in these instances we must disclose our suspicions, normally in the first instance to our supervisor. Of course, this may be an innocent set of transactions but if there is a suspicion of money laundering the least ethical action would be to keep quiet about the issue.

Activity 7: Report to whom? (1)

	✓
National Crime Agency (NCA)	
The police	
Your firm's nominated officer (providing they are not your manager)	✓

As you are working for a large accounting practice there should be a nominated officer to whom your suspicions can be internally reported. The nominated officer can then take the decision to take further action as required, which may mean then reporting externally to the National Crime Agency (NCA). This situation is delicate as the individual reported upon is your manager, however there does seem to be evidence of money laundering taking place here, and therefore needs to be disclosed.

Activity 8: Report to whom? (2)

	✓
National Crime Agency (NCA)	✓
The client	
Nominated officer for money laundering reports	

As you are a sole trader you will not have a nominated officer, so you would need to report externally to the National Crime Agency (NCA) using a Suspicious Activity Report (SAR). If the your suspicions was reported to the client this may be seen as tipping off giving the client an opportunity to dispose of any criminal property.

Activity 9: Money laundering – true or false?

Description	True ✓	False ✓
If a sole trader suspects money laundering they must disclose this to their nominated officer.		✓
Conviction of a Money Laundering Regulations offence will give an AAT member a criminal record.	✓	
Telling a client that they have been the subject of a notification to the National Crime Agency (NCA) could amount to the criminal offence of tipping off.	✓	

Activity 10: Appropriate action

You would like to check that your suspicions (that the employee is being paid cash so they and the employer avoid tax liabilities) are well-founded, but you are aware of the danger of **'tipping off'** the client.

This type of activity is known as concealing a tax liability, because funds which are rightfully HMRC's are being retained by the business and the employee, and it is a form of money laundering.

As a relevant person in a regulated sector you may have to make a protected report to your firm's nominated officer, although the internal rules of your practice may mean you should report it to the partner in charge of the client before doing so.

Activity 11: Tax return and appropriate action

(a) In this situation, James is acting as an ⬛ **agent** of Brian Ltd. Brian Ltd is the ⬛ **principal** .

(b) James is obliged to report the client's refusal and the facts surrounding it to ⬛ **the Money Laundering Reporting Officer** .

Activity 12: Tax savings

	✓
Provide them with an estimate based on what you achieved last year.	
Tell them that you will save them as much as possible.	
Tell them that you cannot provide such information.	✓

Activity 13: Significant tax errors

	✓
Do nothing as admitting errors will damage your professional reputation.	
Correct the error by adjusting this year's tax return to compensate.	
Tell the client to advise HMRC about the error.	✓

Activity 14: Whistleblowing and appropriate actions

(a)

Description	True ✓	False ✓
The manager's behaviour is in the interests of the public.		✓
Anna's ability to work with the appropriate level of professional competence and due care is being compromised.	✓	
Providing she acts in good faith she will be protected under the Public Interest Disclosure Act.	✓	

(b)

Action	Steps in sequential order
Initial action	Report internally (where procedures exist)
If further action is needed	Report externally

Test your learning: answers

Chapter 1 – The principles of ethical working

1   The correct answer is:

	✓
True	
False	✓

Group values are very important, eg in families and friendship groups (which is where we get our ideas from), national cultures and organisations (which establish ethical norms and expectations by which we have to operate).

2   The correct answer is:

	✓
Enhance the reputation and standing of accountants.	✓
Limit the number of members that it has.	
Make sure that accountants are able to earn large salaries.	

The accountancy profession needs to maintain standards of conduct and service among its members in order to be able to enhance the reputation and standing of all accountants (so that, for example, they are able to attract and retain clients).

3   The correct answer is:

	✓
Failure to keep up to date on CPD.	
A personal financial interest in the client's affairs.	✓
Being negligent or reckless with the accuracy of the information provided to the client.	

A personal financial interest in the client's affairs will affect objectivity. Failure to keep up to date on CPD is an issue of professional competence, while providing inaccurate information reflects upon professional integrity.

4   The correct answer is:

	✓
Say that you will get back to him when you have looked up the answer.	
Give him the contact details of a friend in your firm who knows all about accounting standards.	
Clarify the limits of your expertise with the client.	✓

This is an issue of technical competence and due care. You should clarify the limits of your expertise with the client, and **then** seek information or guidance from the relevant source.

5   The correct answer is:

Apply safeguards to eliminate or reduce the threat to an acceptable level.	3
Evaluate the seriousness of the threat.	2
Discontinue the action or relationship giving rise to the threat.	4
Identify a potential threat to a fundamental ethical principle.	1

The procedure is laid out in the conceptual framework but members are encouraged to seek external advice where required.

6   The correct answer is:

	✓
It is in the public interest that accountants who fail to comply with standards are taken to court.	
It is in the public interest that accountancy services are carried out to professional standards.	✓

It is in the public interest that accountancy services are performed to professional standards, but failure to do so will not result in an accountant being taken to court. Instead the professional body may take action itself against the accountant under its internal rules.

7 The correct answer is:

Rotation of personnel	✓
Having an employee share scheme	
Use of ethic committees	✓
Use of professional judgement	✓
Encouraging staff to cycle to work	

8 The correct answer is:

	✓
Economic (financial)	✓
Marketing	
Environmental	✓
Charity	
Social	✓
Political	

9 The correct answer is:

	✓
Reputational	
Litigation	
Process	
People	✓
Systems	
Legal	
Event	

The definition is that of people risk.

10 The correct answer is:

	✓
True	
False	✓

Accountants are only expected to keep themselves up to date in areas of accountancy relevant to their everyday work.

Chapter 2 – Behaving in an ethical manner – part I

1   The correct answer is:

	✓
True	
False	✓

Discovery of a significant error while re-evaluating your work gives rise to a self-review threat.

2   The correct answer is:

	✓
Self-interest	✓
Self-review	
Advocacy	
Familiarity	
Intimidation	

A self-interest threat is created as you now have an interest in the transaction.

3   The correct answer is:

	✓
Providing a second opinion	✓
Accepting a gift from a supplier	

Providing a second opinion creates a threat to the fundamental principle of professional competence and due care as you may not be aware of all the information you might need to form a second opinion.

4

	✓
The Bribery Act 2010	
The Terrorism Act 2000	✓

Anti-money laundering legislation in the UK consists of the Terrorism Act 2000, the Proceeds of Crime Act 2002, and the Money Laundering Regulations 2007 (as amended).

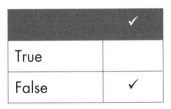

5   The correct answer is:

	✓
A process undertaken before taking on a new engagement to identify any potential threats to the fundamental principles	✓
Keeping up to date in knowledge and skills and ensuring work is completed with accuracy	

Due diligence is a procedure that is carried out before accepting engagements from new clients or accepting new engagements from existing clients. The purpose of this process is to identify any threats to the ethical principles or identify any other reasons why the engagement should be accepted. One specific risk is the possibility that money laundering may be involved.

Chapter 3 – Behaving in an ethical manner – part II

1 The correct answer is:

	✓
Self-interest	✓
Self-review	
Advocacy	
Familiarity	

Accepting gifts and hospitality from a client can give rise to self-interest and intimidation threats to objectivity.

2 Being bribed | is | an offence under the Bribery Act 2010.

The three other offences under this legislation are bribing another person, bribing a foreign public official and failure by a commercial organisation to prevent bribery.

3 The correct answer is:

	✓
True	✓
False	

Failure to notify is an offence under the Data Protection Act.

4 The correct answer is:

	✓
True	✓
False	

Your duty means that you must always respect the confidentiality of information of ex-clients and employers.

5

	✓
True	✓
False	

Disclosures in the public interest are a valid reason to breach confidentiality.

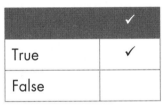

Chapter 4 – Taking appropriate action

1   The correct answer is:

	✓
One of the accountant's employees with ethics training.	
The ethics advice line of their professional body or a close friend.	
An independent legal expert or the ethics advice line of their professional body.	✓

Employees or close friends should not be asked due to confidentiality issues.

2   The correct answer is:

	✓
5 years	✓
7 years	
14 years	

The anti-money laundering legislation makes tipping off an offence, the maximum penalty for which is five years imprisonment or an unlimited fine.

3   The correct answer is:

	✓
The client	✓
The accountant	

The client is responsible for the accuracy of facts, information and computations used in the tax work done by the accountant.

4   The correct answer is:

	✓
Your profession and HMRC	
Your employer and your client	
Your employer, your profession and the public interest	✓

An accountant has a responsibility to further the legitimate aims of their employer, profession and the public interest.

5   The correct answer is:

	✓
Terminate the appointment at once.	
Refuse.	✓
Report your client to the relevant authorities.	

The request may have been made in ignorance and good faith, so you should attempt to explain the technical, legal and ethical principles that apply.

Glossary of terms

It is useful to be familiar with interchangeable terminology including IFRS and UK GAAP (generally accepted accounting principles).

Below is a short list of the most important terms you are likely to use or come across, together with their international and UK equivalents.

UK term	International term
Profit and loss account	**Statement of profit or loss (or statement of profit or loss and other comprehensive income)**
Turnover or Sales	Revenue or Sales Revenue
Operating profit	Profit from operations
Reducing balance depreciation	Diminishing balance depreciation
Depreciation/depreciation expense(s)	Depreciation charge(s)
Balance sheet	**Statement of financial position**
Fixed assets	Non-current assets
Net book value	Carrying amount
Tangible assets	Property, plant and equipment
Stocks	Inventories
Trade debtors or Debtors	Trade receivables
Prepayments	Other receivables
Debtors and prepayments	Trade and other receivables
Cash at bank and in hand	Cash and cash equivalents
Long-term liabilities	Non-current liabilities
Trade creditors or creditors	Trade payables
Accruals	Other payables
Creditors and accruals	Trade and other payables
Capital and reserves	Equity (limited companies)
Profit and loss balance	Retained earnings
Cash flow statement	**Statement of cash flows**

Accountants often have a tendency to use several phrases to describe the same thing! Some of these are listed below:

Different terms for the same thing
Nominal ledger, main ledger or general ledger
Subsidiary ledgers, memorandum ledgers
Subsidiary (sales) ledger, sales ledger
Subsidiary (purchases) ledger, purchases ledger

Bibliography

Association of Accounting Technicians (2014) *Disciplinary Regulations*. [Online]. Available from: https://www.aat.org.uk/prod/s3fs-public/assets/Disciplinary_Regulations.pdf [Accessed 1 May 2018].

Association of Accounting Technicians (2017) *AAT Code of Professional Ethics*. [Online] Available from: https://www.aat.org.uk/prod/s3fs-public/assets/AAT-Code-Professional-Ethics.pdf [Accessed 1 May 2018].

Basel Committee on Banking Supervision (2011) *Principles for the Sound Management of Operational Risk*. Basel, Bank for International Settlements.

Bribery Act 2010. (2010) London, TSO.

Committee on Standards in Public Life (1995) *The 7 principles of public life*. [Online]. Available from: https://www.gov.uk/government/publications/the-7-principles-of-public-life [Accessed 10 May 2017].

Data Protection Act 2018. (2018) London, TSO.

EU GDPR Portal (2018). *EU GDPR Information Portal* [online] Available at: https://www.eugdpr.org/ [Accessed 10 May 2018].

FRC (2016) *Ethical Standard* [Online]. Available from: https://www.frc.org.uk/getattachment/0bd6ee4e-075c-4b55-a4ad-b8e5037b56c6/Revised-Ethical-Standard-2016-UK.pdf [Accessed 1 May 2018].

Fraud Act 2006. (2006) London, TSO.

Goldsmith, S. K. and Samson, D. A. (2005) *Sustainable Development and Business Success: Reaching Beyond the Rhetoric to Superior Business Performance*. Sydney, Australian Business Foundation.

Institute of Business Ethics (2012) [Online]. Available from: https://www.ibe.org.uk [Accessed 3 April 2012].

Money Laundering, Terrorist Financing and Transfer of Funds (Information on the Payer) Regulations 2017. (2017) SI 2017/692. London, The Stationery Office.

Proceeds of Crime Act 2002. (2002) London, TSO.

Public Interest Disclosure Act 1998. (1998) London, TSO.

Terrorism Act 2000. (2000) London, TSO.

World Commission on Environment and Development (1987) *Our Common Future.* Oxford, New York, Oxford University Press.

Index

REVIEW FORM

How have you used this Course Book?
(Tick one box only)

☐ Self study

☐ On a course_____

☐ Other _____

Why did you decide to purchase this Course Book? *(Tick one box only)*

☐ Have used BPP materials in the past

☐ Recommendation by friend/colleague

☐ Recommendation by a college lecturer

☐ Saw advertising

☐ Other _____

During the past six months do you recall seeing/receiving either of the following?
(Tick as many boxes as are relevant)

☐ Our advertisement in Accounting Technician

☐ Our Publishing Catalogue

Which (if any) aspects of our advertising do you think are useful?
(Tick as many boxes as are relevant)

☐ Prices and publication dates of new editions

☐ Information on Course Book content

☐ Details of our free online offering

☐ None of the above

Your ratings, comments and suggestions would be appreciated on the following areas of this Course Book.

	Very useful	Useful	Not useful
Chapter overviews	☐	☐	☐
Introductory section	☐	☐	☐
Quality of explanations	☐	☐	☐
Illustrations	☐	☐	☐
Chapter activities	☐	☐	☐
Test your learning	☐	☐	☐
Keywords	☐	☐	☐

	Excellent	Good	Adequate	Poor
Overall opinion of this Course Book	☐	☐	☐	☐

Do you intend to continue using BPP Products?   ☐ Yes ☐ No

Please note any further comments and suggestions/errors on the reverse of this page. The BPP author of this edition can be emailed at: lmfeedback@bpp.com.

Alternatively, the Head of Programme of this edition can be emailed at: nisarahmed@bpp.com.

REVIEW FORM (continued)

TELL US WHAT YOU THINK

Please note any further comments and suggestions/errors below